Redeeming A Father's Heart

Men Share Powerful Stories of Abortion Loss and Recovery

Kevin Burke LSW,
David Wemhoff,
Marvin Stockwell

AuthorHouse™
1663 Liberty Drive, Suite 200
Bloomington, IN 47403
www.authorhouse.com
Phone: 1-800-839-8640

First published by AuthorHouse 5/22/2007

ISBN: 978-1-4343-1367-6 (sc)

Printed in the United States of America
Bloomington, Indiana
This book is printed on acid-free paper.

Dedication

*To the countless children
Longing to be known, loved and embraced
In their Father's Hearts.*

Acknowledgements

Thanks To:

David Wemhoff who provided the support, leadership, editorial skills, and friendship that were essential for this to come together.

Marvin Stockwell who was an invaluable and talented editor and friend throughout the project.

Janet Morana, co-founder of the Silent No More Awareness Campaign, who planted the mustard seed that grew into this powerful collection of stories.

Andrea Staarguard for her work on the cover.

Katie D'Annunzio for her faithful service to family and ministry.

Patti Baratta, Linda Renken, and Pam Robinson for proofing and editing assistance.

Fr Frank Pavone and Priests For Life for their ongoing support as we work together to build a Culture of Life.

Theresa my beautiful wife for her continual encouragement to respond to God's will in my life, and especially for her partnership with the Holy Spirit in developing the powerful post abortion healing process of *Rachel's Vineyard* and *Grief to Grace*. The healing retreats Theresa developed are changing the lives of men and women around the world …but the greatest gift she has given me is our 5 precious children.

Finally, a special thanks to Mary, the Mother of our Redeemer.

Kevin Burke

Contents

Foreword

Adam!!

It was a sunny morning in the South, but a sad one, as one young mother after another streamed into the abortion facility, occasionally accompanied by the father of the child. I was there with a team of other people to offer hope in despair and alternatives to those who had likely been told there were none.

Occasionally, the quiet morning air was broken by a prayer or a song. Then, at one point in our vigil, a man on our team decided to appeal to the fathers of these children who were scheduled for death. And he called out to them all, giving them one collective name.

"Adam! Adam!!!!" He spoke, as a man to a man, invoking the name of the first man. *"Adam!"* He addressed them with this name, which is more like a title of honor. *"Adam!"* With that cry, this man invoked upon his fellow men the God-given responsibility to protect the life that flows from the Creator and to affirm the woman in whom that life grows.

He reminded them that at the beginning of our history, God set the first man as guardian of the Garden. The man gave names to all created things. Then "woman" was created from his side – an indication of equality – and the two formed the image of God.

Yet before long, we see the serpent lying to the first woman, confusing her, and urging her to disobey God. This, of course, leads to the original sin, which both Adam and Eve commit. There is a disturbing question, however, that we should not pass over. *How did the serpent get into the garden in the first place?*

Adam failed. He was to protect the garden, the woman, and the gifts God had given, which would include their children. But the serpent was able to get in anyway. Somehow, Adam failed in his vigilance. And his name rang out that morning, to remind other men to keep vigilant against the many voices that can lead them astray--and lead to untold grief, regret, and pain in their lives and the lives of the women and children entrusted to them.

That cry rings out again in this book. And in it, you will hear Adam speak. He will speak of his failure and of his God-given responsibilities. He will speak, too, of something even more wondrous: *the New Adam, who redeems every man, brings hope out of despair, and makes all things new.* That Man, who is also the Son of God, has a word to speak to the men of our day. Nowhere is it spoken more effectively than through the testimonies you will read here.

In my ministry as National Director of Priests for Life and Pastoral Director of Rachel's Vineyard, I have met with men in every part of this nation who have learned, by difficult personal experience, that abortion destroys everyone it touches. They have learned that the law, which gives them no right to protect their own child from an abortion, subtly but powerfully says to them that, likewise, they should take no responsibility. They have felt the bitter anger that comes from abortions they could not stop and the overwhelming despair that comes from abortions they insisted upon. They have learned how even abortions in which they had no participation at all have had the power to alter their lives.

They have also learned that in Jesus Christ there is forgiveness, healing, hope, and new manhood.

Today, more men than ever are coming forward as part of a growing multitude of those who have been wounded by abortion. Many of them find healing in quiet and confidential settings with a pastor or counselor; many others experience the tremendous power of a Rachel's Vineyard Retreat and are able to live their lives with greater confidence and peace. Still others have begun speaking publicly about their experiences through the national Silent No More Awareness Campaign. And there are many others, still, who have not found any healing, and whom we strive to reach.

I am profoundly grateful to Kevin Burke, Director of Rachel's Vineyard Ministries, for the outreach he conducts for men. The research he has done, the training he has imparted, and the counseling he offers have lifted many to new levels of awareness and peace. His wife, Dr. Theresa Burke, has likewise done groundbreaking work in healing people after abortion. I am proud to partner with them both.

I salute the men who have shared their stories in this book. I salute them and stand with them as we work together to restore the authentic meaning of manhood and fatherhood amidst a culture that has forgotten and disfigured it. These are not just men who have an experience to share. These are men through whom the New Adam is bringing about a restoration we all seek.

■ *Fr. Frank Pavone, National Pastoral Director, Rachel's Vineyard Ministries*

I was young and so was she
Love didn't stay a mystery for very long
We could do no wrong
Then she called to say
She was late
So we took a little drive upstate
And took care of that
Yeah, we just took care of that

Now I'm looking back on
Some of my decisions
Now that it's much too late to change
How a father could have held his son
If I could undo what's been done
But I guess everyone is living
With water and bridges

- *Water and Bridges*
Tim Nichols and Craig Wiseman

Introduction

*"Abortion is a private, personal decision between a woman,
her health-care provider, and her god."*

It's a catchy sound bite often used by proponents of abortion rights.
But like much of the debate that swirls about this issue, it's totally
disconnected from the real life experiences of men and women who
participate in an abortion procedure.

The reality is that men are intimately involved in the decisions of
their girlfriends, partners and spouses to have an abortion. In 95% of all
cases a man plays a central role in the decision of a woman to abort. [1]

Society tells us that men are quite comfortable with the abortion
option, and have little, if any, problems after the procedure. On the
surface it would seem so. But dig a little deeper and, like Drexel
University Sociology Professor Arthur Shostak, you may be surprised
by what you discover.

In the early seventies, Arthur Shostak accompanied his lover to a
suburban abortion clinic. They had both agreed that abortion was the
only sensible solution to their situation and scheduled an appointment
for the procedure. The level of pain and discomfort he experienced
that day as he sat in that waiting room shocked him.

Shostak spent the next ten years studying the abortion experiences
of men. His study included a survey of 1,000 men who accompanied
wives or girlfriends to abortion centers.[2] Shostak found that one in

---

[1] Mary K Zimmerman, *Passage Through Abortion* (Praeger, 1978).
[2] Arthur Shostak, *Men and Abortion: Lessons, Losses and Love* (Praeger, 1984).

four men considered abortion to be a participation in the death of their unborn child. Slightly over 80% said they had already started to think about the child that might have been born (29% think of the child "frequently"). Many cried during the interview process.

Newsweek magazine featured a February, 2007 cover story entitled "Men and Depression." The article revealed that men suffer much higher rates of depression than previously thought. Irritability, anger management issues, and addictions are some of the ways that many men give voice to their painful feelings of sadness. Unfortunately many counselors, pastors, friends and family fail to make a connection between these uniquely male symptoms and a deepening depression.

Terrence Real points out in his important book on male depression, *I Don't Want To Talk About It,*[3] that men have the capacity to deeply repress areas of loss and pain. Facing these feelings leads to a sense of vulnerability, loss of control and weakness that men perceive as more *feminine* emotions that are to be avoided at all cost.

So in an effort to hide from these emotions, many men throw themselves into work, addictions, pornography, affairs…anything to escape this vulnerability. Tragically such escapes and attempts to maintain control exacts a high price over time as relationships become dysfunctional, marriage and family life suffer, and productivity as well as performance decreases.

The stories in *Redeeming A Father's Heart* reveal that for many men abortion is a traumatic experience of loss, involving exposure to and participation in what is viewed as a death event. Whether this loss is conscious, or buried deep in the unconscious, men will experience anger, guilt and shame rooted in the "complicated grief" [4] from their participation in abortion. This complicated mourning, shame and guilt leave men vulnerable to some of the classic symptoms of male depression, irritability, anger, negativity and criticism, abuse of drugs/alcohol, withdrawal from loved ones, difficulty concentrating, eat and sleep disturbances and sexual dysfunction. [5]

---

[3] Terrence Real, *I Don't Want to Talk About It* (Scribner, 1998).

[4] Persons experiencing complicated grief or mourning are unable to progress in the natural mourning process to a place of acceptance and resolution.

[5] Thomas Strahan, "Portraits of Post-Abortive Fathers Devastated by the Abortion Experience," *Assoc. for Interdisciplinary Research in Values and Social Change,* 7(3), Nov/Dec 1994.

But despite this suffering, men struggle to reach out for the help they so desperately need. They can find themselves gasping for air as repressed emotions rise up with a vengeance pulling them toward what feels like a terrifying dark abyss. Without medical treatment and a process for spiritual and emotional healing, men are at risk for emotional illness, stress related physical ailments such as heart disease and stroke and tragically, suicide. [6]

I can assure you from my experience as Associate Director of Rachel's Vineyard, an international post abortion healing ministry of Priests For Life, that each of the stories in *Redeeming A Father's Heart* represents countless wounded men. In the last year alone, nearly 500 Rachel's Vineyard Weekend retreats were offered around the world for men and women suffering after abortion. Each experience of abortion is unique, but we find some common themes.

Sadly, many men resort to various forms of manipulation, withdrawal of emotional and physical support, and even outright aggression to present abortion to their girlfriends and wives as the only solution to an unplanned pregnancy. A number of the stories in this book reveal how deeply painful it is when men face the truth of their role in an abortion decision. But it is an essential step in their healing and recovery.

Yet other men stand ready to embrace fatherhood, regardless of the circumstances. These men have no "choice" in the abortion decision and find themselves powerless to save the life of their child. They are especially vulnerable after the abortion as they encounter potentially life threatening rage and grief and need immediate support and healing resources. (See Chapter Six, "Prison of Ice", and Chapter Four, "My Abortion Story: A Father's Perspective".)

Many husbands are profoundly affected by abortion, though never directly involved in an abortion decision. These men married women with an abortion in their past (this is often a closely guarded secret). You may be surprised to learn the powerful impact a previous abortion has on the emotional, physical and spiritual intimacy between a husband and wife. (Chapter Three, "I Married A Post Abortive Woman".)

I have learned through my counseling and retreat ministry that many men enter relationships with women deeply wounded from divorce;

---

[6] Though more women attempt suicide, more men die from suicide in part because men use more lethal methods such as firearms, and act more quickly on suicidal thoughts. (*Newsweek*, "Men and Depression," February 26, 2007)

absent, distant or abusive fathers; previous sexual abuse, and other losses. When faced with an unplanned pregnancy, these men struggle with fear and a sense of inadequacy at the prospects of embracing fatherhood. This leaves them vulnerable to seeing abortion as the best solution to their situation.

After abortion, they struggle to reconcile the pain and rejection they experienced as children with their own failure to accept and protect the life of their son or daughter in the womb. The abortion loss connects with unresolved feelings of rage and grief from childhood complicating and intensifying their post abortion reactions. (Chapter Two, "Deadly Perfectionism".)

The stories of loss and recovery in *Redeeming a Father's Heart*, and the millions of men they represent, speak their truth more effectively than any statistic or study. We present the powerful stories of these courageous men who had the humility and strength rooted in forgiveness and healing to share their stories. I have the greatest respect for these men and deepest gratitude for their important gift. They share a common desire to present the truth of their abortion experience and the consequences of this choice. You will read how important healing has been for their personal, relational, and spiritual health as men, fathers, spouses and friends.

You may have picked up this book and have an abortion in your past…read on! I promise this little book will change your life. You may be married to a man touched by abortion and in need of healing. After you read these stories you will have a greater appreciation for the unique experience of male post abortion grief. Share *Redeeming A Father's Heart* with friends, husbands, boyfriends, parents, brothers and any man or woman touched by abortion. Give this book to the counselors, clergy, and medical professionals who may encounter suffering men with abortion in their history, and who need to understand the importance of emotional and spiritual healing of this loss.

It is my hope and prayer that this book will provide a voice for the countless men who struggle in silent isolation to understand their inner pain. They may appear successful and in control, but beneath the surface there is an experience of loss, shame and guilt that cries out for repentance and release and a heart that longs for reconciliation and peace.

Some of these stories will be hard reading initially, especially if they touch upon areas of your own personal story. Stay with it, because ultimately *Redeeming A Father's Heart* reveals that nothing is beyond the capacity of God to heal and redeem.

I pray these stories will be a special roadmap for you, pointing the way to deeper understanding, hope and healing.

Kevin Burke, MSS/LSW
March, 2007

Chapter One
The Continuing Healing

By Jonathan Flora

*"If you look for truth, you may find comfort in the end;
if you look for comfort you will not get either comfort or
truth only soft soap and wishful thinking to begin, and in
the end, despair." - C. S. Lewis*

Spring 2006. I was in Orlando, Florida to speak at an International Pro-Life Conference. About one o'clock that afternoon, I started losing my voice.

By the time of the event, my voice had not returned but I was able to get through it. The audience took it in stride, albeit with a thin slice of amusement. I opened my talk by telling the nearly 500 attendees about a phone conversation I had with my 2 ½ year-old daughter Olivia, earlier that afternoon. When she didn't recognize my voice, I tried to explain to her why I sounded the way I did. I said, "Daddy is hoarse."

And she responds by saying, "Neigh." I then proceeded to go through eight or nine other barnyard animal sounds with her. The audience laughed. I smiled. But on the inside, I was nearly moved to tears. Tears of love and gratitude. I am so grateful and so blessed to even have a daughter so a moment like this could take place. And, I could share it with others.

I will always remember 2006 as a whirlwind of appearances, speaking engagements, meetings, and conferences, starting off as a keynote speaker with my wife Deborah, for the 33rd March For Life in Washington, D.C. Since becoming involved in the pro-life movement, I have heard many heartbreaking testimonies from women who've experienced abortions. Many of them, sadly, had multiple abortions. Almost always, these women refer to the guy in their life that played a critical role in their decision to have an abortion. Often, the guy played a forceful, coercive role.

January of that year on a cold day in Washington, D.C., I was standing in front of the Supreme Court Building. I was moments away from speaking publicly for the first time about my abortion experience when it suddenly hit me.

I was, "the guy."

1978-79. The Jonestown Massacre took place, as did the first test tube baby (in-vitro fertilization), the Susan B. Anthony dollar coin was weaved into circulation, Skylab fell into the Indian Ocean, Iranian students stormed the U.S. Embassy and held 52 people hostage for 444 days, the Soviet Union invaded Afghanistan, the Walkman was introduced, Three Mile Island had a partial meltdown, and Ultrasound was first used. Lost within all those world events was me - and millions of others - just living our everyday lives.

I was driving a silver 1973 Ford Mustang, the last year of its greatness as a king of street muscle cars. I was back in Ohio, having just received an Honorable Discharge from the U.S. Army's 82d Airborne Division. And with the already five years of success of Paul McCartney's "new" band, Wings, I was finally accepting the dreaded reality that The Beatles would never get back together. Tragically, less than a year later that reality would be finalized with the assassination of John Lennon.

Back in Ohio, I was also heading off to college. This was an exciting time for me and the beginning of yet another new chapter in my life. For the first time I felt free of my father's restrictions that came along with a disciplined and firm military lifestyle as well as my own experience in the Army.

Although I was raised as a Christian, I had no real relationship with God. In the military you get two flavors; Catholic and everything else that is lumped into the Protestant category. We were the latter.

However, when my father retired from a career in the Navy and returned with us to his home state of Ohio, we attended a "fire and brimstone" church. I was taught God's way is hard and exact. To fall short of His law is to experience His wrath of which He is quick to deliver. I didn't want that from my earthly father, so why would I voluntarily serve a heavenly Father described as the same?

I left religion behind when I enlisted in the Army four years earlier, and now felt truly free of the shackles of forced adherence within the strictness of another's rules. Now nothing stood in my way. I alone would choose how I would, or be allowed, to live.

If no one is getting hurt (so we thought), and if it feels good, do it. And I did. What I didn't realize at the time however, is freedom in reality is not defined as being able to do whatever one wants. Freedom comes with responsibilities and consequences, and free will comes with the option to run from them.

Of course, free "love" isn't free, and of course, I got a girl pregnant. No problem, I thought, this was just a speed bump. Several options presented themselves immediately. Agreeing we did not want anyone else to know she was pregnant, we quickly eliminated all but one - abortion.

In my eyes my future remained clear. One of us was in love and it wasn't me. I knew what needed to be done. I bought into the multitude of lies that our society so eagerly spread and my government and lawmakers had so readily deemed "best" for me. No problem, no guilt. All I had to do was write an inexpensive check and that "problem" would easily go away.

I was looking for comfort when I should have been seeking the truth. Instead, I regurgitated the same lies and used all the common excuses to not live up to my responsibility; I was in college, too young (she was even younger), no money, in no way ready to be a father, and again, I knew she and I had no future together.

The lie that sealed the deal? It's only a "blob of tissue. It's not a baby until sometime later," I was told. However, no one could tell me exactly when that time was. This dehumanizing of the baby was the biggest lie of all. This final lie closed the deal on how I was able to completely disconnect from the truth of what was about to take place and decide to have the abortion.

By being "the guy" I had the advantage of being able to separate myself from another critical reality. You see, I was not the one that would have to go through the actual abortion procedure. I would never be haunted by the faces of those in the abortion clinic, the impersonal, shallow words spoken, the smells, the colors of the room, the sounds. None of the sight, sound, feel, and experiences of the procedure that I have heard so many women describe in such intricate detail. I simply had to drive my girlfriend to the clinic, write the check, and pick her up afterward. And that's exactly what I did. I didn't even wait at the facility for her. I just picked her up afterward.

I don't remember what I did between the time I dropped her off and picked her up. I can't visualize what the building looked like. I don't recall what kind of day it was, sunny, cloudy, cold, hot. I do know, we never talked about it during the drive back. Or ever. We broke up soon after. Even though we saw each other occasionally, we never got back together.

For nearly two decades, I never spoke about the abortion. Not a word. I'm not sure it was even a conscious decision. I simply didn't speak of it. Whether I was aware or unaware that this is an emotional pattern seemingly developed for protection, it served just the opposite. In reality, I simply suffered in silence from the deep wounds unseen and numbed, hidden and unresolved, even though my lifestyle and attitude screamed of them. I can't tell you this led me to drugs because we all smoked pot and took other things back then and of course, we drank. But I can tell you, it didn't make me stop any of that either.

Following our break up, my attitude with women became even more emotionally detached. I never really allowed myself to get too close. Even though I may have tried to talk myself into believing I had a deep affection, girls were primarily for physical companionship only. Even in those rare instances where I did experience deeper emotions, devotion and loyalty were soon not included. Because of this, there was never any real commitment. This always made it easier to move on.

For me, making and breaking relationships was easy – I had done it my whole life. I learned early and it was all I knew growing up. Because of my father's Naval career, I attended seven different schools (two outside the U.S.) from first grade through my senior year in high school. I was never at one school for more than three years and those were my last three. I can't imagine how many classmates I had over those years. Because military kids were always moving, maybe a third or less of the class that started the year together would be intact by the time summer break rolled around. Making and breaking relationships was easy.

If it was easy to start and end relationships with friends and classmates as a kid, later in life breaking up with girls was handled just as easily. In fact, having "the talk" with them was more difficult for me than making the actual decision to end the relationship. Too often, I even ran from "the talk." Another escape from responsibility.

When dating someone, it was easy to cheat, and easy to lie to cover it up. Once I started telling, believing, and living lies, it became more and more normal to me. Reality is what I created, not caring that it was totally self-manufactured. And if a girl cheated on me, it just reinforced my belief that no one is to be trusted, including myself. My life was an emotional façade. I was on the downward spiral with no boundaries and I was oblivious to what was happening to me.

The downward spiral with no boundaries. Here's how it works. If you never trust anyone, you'll never really love. If you don't love, you're never vulnerable. If you're never vulnerable, you can't get hurt. If you can't get hurt, you are immune. If you're immune, you can do anything. If you can do anything, you can do no wrong. But, here's the kicker. If you can do no wrong, then that means nothing is right. And if nothing is right, what is good? What is there to be valued and cherished? Nothing. The line that separates right and wrong becomes blurred and is soon erased. The distinction between the two is lost, hidden within those well-crafted lies. That's the genius of deceit. Within its complexity, it's all very simple. But, you have to get off the downward spiral to be able to see it.

Feeding the emotional deficit with counterfeit, physical "food" like drugs or sex devoid of emotional investment, never satisfies. Like any vice, it doesn't take long before you discover it takes twice the stimulation to feel half as good as the last time. So you take or do more to feed the emotional craving and stimulate the physical desire. You keep pushing the envelope until something breaks. Here's another deceit, sometimes, often, you don't even know you're broken. Hopefully, you find out before it's too late.

1990 and now nearly 40 years old. I was director of marketing and corporate sponsorships for an extremely successful worldwide sports entertainment company located on the east coast. I helped sell out stadiums and coliseums in the U.S., Europe and Canada, sometimes in a matter of hours. What did I have to show for it? I knew something was wrong but I couldn't put my finger on it. Forget the exciting job and all the traveling. Forget the nice car. Forget the girls. I had nothing of any real value to be proud of or to cherish.

My walk in the wilderness was half as long as the people of Israel but still, twenty years is plenty long enough.

Where was God in all this? Right where He always is, smack dab in front of me. But I had my head down, glued to the path I was determined to travel. As a result, I was too distracted and obsessed to see Him. Also, by now I had been lost for far too long to still be calling out His name in hopes of being found and in turn rescued.

Still, Jesus is the truth and God has a plan for us whether we are experiencing Him or not.

1997 and now living in California. I moved to Los Angeles three years earlier and was still easily making and breaking relationships. One day I was working out in the gym when something unexpected happened. An attractive girl who was a personal trainer sat next to me while I was stretching. I'd seen her around for years even though we never really spoke.

But on this day, right away she started talking to me. She told me she had just broken up with her boyfriend. How convenient. I just broke up with a girl, so the timing was perfect, but not at all for what I thought. She told me that even though she was still hurting from the breakup, a church she was going to was really helping her. Before I knew what happened, the words, "what church?" came out of my mouth. Even though on the inside I had hit "pause" so I could stop to try and figure out what had just happened or why I asked that, she told me the name and location of the church. We agreed to meet the following Sunday.

Sunday came and to my surprise, I found myself looking forward to it. I was also aware enough to know my anticipation wasn't just to see this girl. While it puzzled me, it also interested me, teasing my curiosity.

As soon as I walked in the church, I was immediately aware of something different. It was nothing physical with the building, no special architecture, colors, sounds, or smells. It was something bigger, much deeper than anything on the surface. Something was present that I had never felt before. I didn't recognize it, but I was in God's presence. Powerful yet peaceful. I sat near the back, telling myself it was so I could see the girl when she walked in. I could also make a quick getaway if necessary.

Three things happened. The girl never showed up, I never left, and God touched me. He spoke to me through one of those sermons that you know was meant only for you. There could have been no one else in the sanctuary; the message was that exact and personal. I broke down in tears. I rededicated myself to the Lord and asked Him for His forgiveness. I admit, it was so overwhelming that when I left the church I was a little confused as to what exactly had just taken place. Still, I knew something very powerful had happened. It felt right and it felt right deep inside.

For the first time in two decades, I truly felt alive and on so many levels. I was a structure going through a serious overhaul. Of course, to this day and always, I remain a work in progress. But I knew, if I was going to go through this change and give this God - this loving, forgiving and compassionate God that I had finally met - a real chance, I had to discipline myself. I could not give Him that chance to fully commit to me if I was not fully committed to Him. If this failed, it would be my fault not His.

I went cold turkey. No dating. No girls. No sex. Wow.

I was learning how to pray to God and the first time, I was having a relationship with Him. I was being taught how to walk in faith and learning how to get into His word and most of all, understand it, not just recite it. Still, I did not speak to anyone about my abortion. There was no real avenue and I was too ashamed to bring it forward on my own. Abortion wasn't really discussed. Therefore, no support groups existed. No invitation was offered.

So, I brought my burden to God directly. I asked Him for His forgiveness and He gave it immediately. Now it was up me. I had to learn to accept it. That took time. I had others pray over me for emotional healing (even though they did not know exactly what for).

But, I knew God knew. I knew He was doing a work in me and I had to let Him. I struggled to allow myself to accept being worthy of His forgiveness. My heart had been closed. The scars were thick and calloused. The wounds were deep and had been buried for a long, long time.

God is patient. God is consistent. God is always there. He understood me better than I understood myself. He knew that just as important as me accepting His forgiveness, was for me to forgive myself. But how could I do that after what I had done? I murdered a child. Not just any child. My child. This baby did nothing wrong except come to be as a result of my reckless lifestyle. The most innocent of the innocent. No semantics, no excuses, no lies, can defend it or describe it as anything other than that. I murdered my son or daughter, then ran.

I now had a choice to make. Revert back to the slow emotional and spiritual death I had been slugging toward. Or submit. I had already experienced one option for over twenty years. It was time to give the alternative a try.

The healing. The firing of iron that needs to be hammered and reshaped and given a new purpose. It's a painful process because it's so focused and direct. The blacksmith, striking accurate blows right at the heart of the matter. The fire, purifying. And eventually, the cool water washing away the debris and impurities. What remains, is an open, vulnerable heart, for the first time in so long, willing to trust. And in turn, be healed.

God had given me a fresh start, a new beginning for all the things yet to come. This was a circle so unlike the downward spiral. I was forgiven by God, which allowed me to forgive myself, which allowed me to accept His forgiveness.

Just as I carried my shame in silence, for a long period of time I carried my healing the same - hidden. There's an element of perceived safety in silence. While I now had God's and my forgiveness, there was still the fear of condemnation from others. In my way of thinking, carrying my healing in silence protected it from being stolen from me. I would later learn differently, that breaking the silence is a major step to healing.

While God is everything, He also uses other people. I was not aware of retreats such as Rachel's Vineyard and groups like The Silent No More Awareness Campaign. Instead, I went at this one-on-one with God. I cannot stress enough the importance and value of the two organizations mentioned above (and others). Men need to put their pride aside. Men need to talk it out. Men need to know that they are not alone and it is not a sign of weakness to admit it. I didn't have that until much later. I wish I had. But, I reached out to God and found His hand extended toward me in grace.

Two years later I was given the opportunity to teach Sunday School for first and second graders. Naively, I volunteered thinking it would be me who would make a difference. However, it was the kids that did so much for me. These young, enthusiastic children, full of laughter, curiosity, and life (and mischief), taught me so much. They taught me how a man can be strong, yet gentle, and never confusing tenderness for weakness. Through them, I now understood for the first time what it meant to be a man and not just a testosterone-driven male.

1999, still loving God, the church, and yes, I was still celibate. Believe me, even to this day, it strikes me strange, knowing myself and my history, that I eventually went over three years as a grown man without being with a woman. Thankfully, my reward was on the way.

That November, our church was having a meeting for those in the movie industry. It was an effort for us to meet one another and possibly work together on future projects. I was not planning on going. Now a producer with one of the most successful movie studios in Hollywood, I was busy enough as it was. I sat in my car at the intersection where I could turn right and head home or drive straight, through the intersection toward the church. The light turned green. I drove straight.

Prior to the meeting, I was speaking with a friend when a woman walked through the front door of the church. My life would be changed forever. The world stopped just for us, for me anyway. Even though I had seen her around, it was as if a veil had suddenly been lifted and I was seeing her for the first time. I was floored. I knew something was different, really different. She introduced herself to me and said that we had met before. I didn't remember, but I knew I would never, ever, forget her again.

We were married eight months later.

2000, with both us marrying for the first time and a bit later in life, we knew our honeymoon as a just a couple would be brief. We both wanted children. Before we were married, I shared my story with her and she cried. She cried for the child that was lost. She cried because I had carried this burden alone for so long and had survived. But she also shed tears of joy for the love she has for God and His mercy. Without my asking, but subconsciously hoping, she immediately forgave me. This was the first time I truly shared my abortion with someone else. The healing continued.

2003, Valentine's Day, my wife called me at work with bad news. The doctor had told her that after nearly two years of trying to get pregnant, he believed we would never have our own children. Knowing my wife was curled up on the couch and crying, I told her that we must praise God in bad times as well as the good, and we did.

But when I hung up the phone, that's when it all came back, crashing on me like a ton of bricks, a thick, dark cloud attempting to suck the life right out of me. "Now what?," I asked. "I praise you God, but am I now being punished for not protecting my first child?" I was not responsible then, how could God ever trust me now? As a man we are called to be the protectors of our family, especially of our young. But as "the guy" I ran from that responsibility. And now, I bore the guilt of denying a second woman her child.

I found myself running again, but this time, back to God. As always, He was there, His arms reaching out to comfort. He is a loving, compassionate, and forgiving Father. I was not being punished. To believe I was, would be buying into another lie. I was done with that. Remember, Jesus is the truth and God has a plan for us whether we are experiencing Him or not. And this time, I was experiencing Him. I have a relationship with Him!

Together my wife and I continued to stand on scripture, especially Exodus 23:25-26, "Worship the Lord your God, and his blessing will be on your food and water. I will take away sickness from among you, and none will miscarry or be barren in your land. I will give you a full life span."

We live in very pluralistic times and with that come many contradictions within our society. During this struggle, that contrast became so obvious and personal to me. Here my wife and I were on our knees praying fervently to God for a child while America is aborting 4,000 babies a day. Based on what? Simply whether the baby is wanted or not wanted. Life had become so devalued that this is how we determined who should live and who should die. The world was still buying into the same lies I did so many years ago.

While doing research on abortions I stumbled across partial-birth abortion. I was shocked when I learned what it was. This was before President Bush has signed the Partial-Birth Abortion Ban. The more research I did on this barbaric procedure, and the more I talked to people who also had never heard of it, or were unclear of the actual process, the more I knew I had to try to bring this issue out. This is when I started writing *A Distant Thunder*.

I know the story for *A Distant Thunder* was put on my heart by God. The wisdom of the world will tell you that you do not make a movie in Hollywood that addresses partial-birth abortion to further your career. The wisdom of God says, "Trust me." I've been asked numerous times if I was afraid to make this movie. Honestly, I was more afraid not to make it. Now I had the opportunity to try and help save other pre-born children through my craft. When we arrive in heaven, we will all be held accountable for not only for what we did with our time here on earth, but also for what we didn't do. I do not want to ever be caught just standing on the sidelines when I could be in the game.

Less than a year before we started shooting *A Distant Thunder*, God proved the doctors wrong and we conceived naturally. My wife gave birth to our daughter Olivia. During the actual shoot, Deborah was 11 weeks pregnant with our son, Benjamin. Miracle gifts from Above! Again, the healing continued.

Not long after the movie was released, I received an e-mail about a young couple at a local college in Los Angeles. They were facing an unwanted pregnancy and had decided to have an abortion. A friend of theirs gave them a DVD of *A Distant Thunder*. God's truth spoke through the movie and their eyes and hearts were opened. As the credits rolled, the guy turned to his girlfriend and said, "We can't do this, let's get married and have this baby." The couple welcomed their new son on Valentine's Day. A wonderful word of encouragement from God.

I was humbled that God used our movie to help another man not become, "the guy."

> *"He raises the poor from the dust and lifts the needy from the ash heap; he seats them with princes." – 1 Samuel 2:8*

2006. Since the release of *A Distant Thunder* I have been blessed to meet with Senators, Congressmen, Governors, and many national leaders. Deborah and I were invited to give presentations for the movie in the Capitol Building in Washington, D.C. and held several screenings on Capitol Hill. We have met with pastors, priests, and leaders of several pro-life organizations and now shoulder with them in this fight. All of us with the common goal; to help others heal, to change hearts and minds, and in turn, rewrite our nation's law so it once again protects God's children. The glacier of truth is beginning to move, but there remains much to do.

God has taken this broken kid from Ohio, and has turned my "choice" and with it, my guilt and shame, into His good.

I have three children. Two are with me. Someday, I will meet my first-born, whom I have named Angela. I shared this with a friend not long ago and his response was, "Not only has your child forgiven you, but she is up there interceding on your behalf." How the healing continues.

I will always be "the guy." But I am also a man that no longer believes the lies and I'm fighting to share the truth. I regret my lost fatherhood. But, I have been forgiven and I will be silent no more.

And, Daddy is still his little girl's favorite horse.

Jonathan Flora is an award-winning producer for a major Hollywood studio and the writer/director of the critically acclaimed movie, A Distant Thunder. For more information, go to www.ADistantThunder.com.

Chapter Two
A Deadly Perfectionism

It was about 3 a.m. when I called my pastor's home, got the answering machine, and left this not so cryptic message, "I just called to say goodbye." I was in the middle of another sleepless night ruminating on how my life had fallen apart. I played judge and jury in this courtroom in my head and kept coming up with the same sentence…Death! I was a complete and abject failure as a man, as a husband and as a father. I couldn't stand the thought of waking up to face another day in my own tortured skin. I hated what my life had become, I hated my weakness and fear, and I hated myself. I told myself with deadly self-pity that everyone I knew would be better off if I was out of the picture.

I meditated once again on the bottle of sleeping medicine on my bedside. Before I could lose nerve I shoved the pills down my throat swallowing them with a can of beer. I lay on my bed and said goodbye to life.

When I came to consciousness I was in the emergency room of a hospital. Thank God, my pastor, Jim, woke from a sound sleep and hearing the phone ring, felt the strong feeling that he should check his answering machine. After hearing my message, he called 911.

Pastor Jim visited me in the hospital once they pumped my stomach and I was out of danger. He told me, "I knew you were going through a tough time, but I didn't realize just how much you were hurting. I hope we can work together to make sure you never see suicide as the only way out."

As I lay in that hospital bed feeling so weak and numb, I wanted to believe that he could help me, but I felt depressed and hopeless. In the days ahead, I began to hope that maybe God, through Pastor Jim's help, had spared my life. There was a reason I had called him; somewhere inside me there was a desire to reach out for help and find healing…but I didn't know how. I started by trying to honestly look at how I got to this point in my life, confined to the psychiatric unit of a hospital on suicide watch.

I grew up in a modest home in a typical suburb in the 1960's. I idolized my father. He was always bigger than life and so much fun to be with. We would go miniature golfing or bowling together. My Mom seemed unhappy a lot of the time, so I really craved my time with Dad. I later learned my Mom was unhappy because she and my father didn't get along. I knew they had fights, and Dad would disappear for a while, but I was usually out playing ball with friends. Despite the marital problems, my father always made time to take me to a ballgame or go out for ice cream on weekends.

I was eight when my Mom told me that she and Dad were getting divorced.   I didn't want to believe it. For a while I pretended it wasn't real. I just believed that any day he would be walking through that door from a business trip. Dad would pick me up like he always did and lift me to the ceiling. He would give me a big hug and kiss and we would wrestle or go out back and throw the football around.

But reality started to settle in, making a mockery of my faith and shattering my denial. I can't begin to explain how devastating it was to lose my Dad. I couldn't wait till those weekends when I could visit him; but they could never replace his presence in my home. Not having him around was the biggest wound. It left a hole in my heart that I could never fill.

My father remarried and had a daughter. More and more of his time and energies went into the new life he was building. I looked forward to my visits, and we did the same fun things, but it wasn't the same. He moved farther away which cut down on visits. He had his new family and I didn't really feel part of my Mom's new family when she remarried. I always felt like an outsider with no place that was truly my home.

As I grew into early adolescence, my mother would frequently tell me that I looked and acted just like my father. I could feel her resentment toward me. She took good care of me, and I am grateful for that. But she was often emotionally distant. I think my presence reminded her of my Dad and her failed first marriage and I could feel that. I am sure she also felt my anger and resentment directed toward her because my Dad left us. She would pick on me and draw me into fights. My stepfather was a nice man who would try to play peacemaker, but in the end, he would inevitably take my Mom's side.

I was considered a good-looking guy, so as I entered adolescence I took solace in the attention of girls, sports and rock music. I partied like most teens in the 70's with some beer and pot now and then, but not to excess. In my last semester of high school I signed up for the Air Force. I was stationed overseas and took advantage of the opportunity to take college courses in business while completing my four years of service. After my discharge, I found an apartment, completed my degree, and went to work for an area corporation that welcomed a veteran with a college degree. My life seemed headed in the right direction, and I felt good about the future.

I met Betsy one night after work at a local club. We danced and hit it off right away. We had only dated for three months when we got engaged. I was really excited to get married. I was lonely, and I hungered to be close to someone and to have a place to call home. I was going to do it right in my life. My kids would never suffer as I did growing up.

Like most engaged couples, we were having sex. It wasn't a regular thing, but once in a while she would stay over, telling her parents she was at a girlfriend's house, and we would sleep together. It never crossed our mind that we might get pregnant since she was on the pill.

One Monday morning at work, Betsy called me. "I'm late for my period and got a pregnancy test," she paused for what seemed like an hour… "I'm pregnant." I couldn't speak! "Aren't you going to say something?" she said. I finally said "I have to get back to a meeting, we can talk about it when I get off work." Needless to say, I didn't get much work done the rest of that day.

In the days ahead, I struggled with feeling that this unplanned pregnancy was not the perfect family thing I envisioned for myself. I didn't want to face our parents and felt embarrassed that we were so stupid. I saw it as a mistake that we needed to fix so we could get on with doing this thing the right way.

I talked to my dad and he reinforced what I was already thinking. He encouraged me to get an abortion saying, "Marriage is tough enough son-you don't want to get off on the wrong foot. Wait 'til you're ready."

Looking back, Betsy was watching my response to the pregnancy very closely. It was a very powerful influence on her decision. Like a lot of women, she wanted to please, and was scared of doing something that would lead me to later resent her or the child. I told Betsy all the rational reasons we should abort:

> *"We don't have a lot of money saved, shouldn't we wait until we are married and settled for a year or so, and find a nice home for us?"*

> *"I'm just thinking of what's best for you and our future family. When we're ready, I want you to have the kind of life you and our children deserve."*

I don't know what was really in Betsy's heart and I made sure that I didn't look deep enough to see anything that might counter my already firm decision. I was set on fixing this problem. Betsy was easily manipulated by my reasoned presentation on why staying pregnant made no sense. I think she was also afraid to let her parents down, but if I had been stronger in wanting to keep the pregnancy, I suspect she would have been happy and relieved.

We scheduled the appointment for the abortion and I took off work so I could go with her. I couldn't wait until the whole thing was over. I stuffed down any doubts that rose up within and told myself that I was doing the right thing, the responsible thing. She came out of the procedure room white as a ghost and said, "Let's get out of here."

I asked how she was, but she wouldn't look at me. She said she felt sick at her stomach and just wanted to get home and go to bed. I didn't know it at the time, but the minute our baby's tiny heart stopped beating that June day in 1983, the seeds of destruction would take deep root in the soil of our relationship and in time would slowly, but surely, yield their toxic fruit.

We didn't see each other for a few days. One of the first things I noticed after the abortion was that we both pretended it never happened. We kept this unspoken pact of silence around the whole business. I also noticed we both drank a bit more when we went out together. As we prepared for our wedding, the momentum of that experience refocused our energies for a time.

We lived in an apartment after the wedding and I began to climb the corporate ladder. I thought of the abortion sometimes. I would have dreams of a phantom male child coming to me but I couldn't see the face; maybe it was me as a boy, or was it my aborted son? Sometimes I would feel depressed about what I had done, but just as quickly I would stuff those feelings down and throw myself into my hyper busy life as a young husband and businessman.

After a few months, Betsy became pregnant and I was overjoyed! Now we could put the past behind us and start building the family I dreamed of. When we went for our first ultrasound appointment I was excited to see the baby. I wondered if it was a boy or girl. It was very exciting when the image came up on the screen. But when I looked over at Betsy she had the same look as the day she walked out of the procedure room at the abortion center; she was white as a ghost and not smiling.

I asked her about it later and she said she was fine and excited about the baby. In the days that followed the ultrasound, I could see that yes, she was excited and planning for her new baby. But there was something else going on inside of her, and I didn't really want to go there. There was so much going on with work, and preparing for our new arrival that I chose to ignore the fact that we were beginning to drift apart ever so slowly.

After the birth of our son, John, Betsy suffered from a serious postpartum depression. Her mom moved in for a while to help out, and with rest and medicine she came out of it. But she just wasn't the same girl I fell in love with when I got out of the service.

It seemed like more and more Betsy never wanted to make love unless she had a few glasses of wine first. I felt like she was going through the motions when we had sex. We were learning to be new parents and all that, but there was something wrong; we were both unhappy and we couldn't talk about it.

I started going out after work now and then with men and women from my office. I would tell Betsy I was working late on some project and might stop for a beer with a few guys from the office. I developed a special friendship with one of the women in this group that I thought we could keep platonic. I had no intention of being unfaithful. Not unexpectedly with both of us drinking, one night we left the bar together, and I ended up going back to her place. After the sex I was overwhelmed with grief and shame for what I had done and vowed to never let it happen again. Unfortunately, I continued to attend the occasional after work party, and we fell into one another's arms again.

Shortly after this, Betsy confronted me after work one day. "When you work late and go out with your buddies for a beer, do any of the women in the office go with you?"

I lied straight to her face. "No, Betsy, it's just some guys from the office," I said. Her expression changed from anger to deep sadness as her eyes brimmed with tears. She mentioned the woman by name! How did she know? It turns out that another co-worker she grew up with heard about the affair and told Betsy about it. I tried to deny there was anything sexual between us, but by now her trust in me was shattered. She knew I was not only unfaithful, but also a liar. She packed up her things and our two-year-old son and went to her mother's home.

I had been living an illusion for some time now – in denial of how unhappy we both were and sliding into the quicksand of the affair. I could not believe that my marriage was falling apart and I was losing my son. The nightmare scenario that I vowed would never happen, was happening. I begged Betsy to come back home, telling her how sorry I was, and vowing to change. She was like a brick wall. She told me her trust in me was shattered, and the marriage was over. It was so final, with no hope of reconciliation or redemption.

My drinking intensified. I would go out after work and try to forget what a mess I made of my life. I starting watching pornography and would go to places for a "massage" that for a fee included sex. This only increased my feelings of shame, disgust and depression. I wanted a home and a family, yet here I was staring at my computer screen as the sewage of Internet porn and cheap chat room sex flowed deep into my soul.

I was seething with rage and self-hatred at what I had done to my life. The drinking and pornography only intensified my feelings of isolation, depression and self-disgust. I thought my son would be better off without a Dad like me. It was shortly after this that I made the suicide attempt.

While I was in the hospital, I met with psychiatrists and counselors in the psychiatric unit. Not one of them asked me if I had an abortion in my history, though we talked about everything else. My pastor was a huge support to me during this very dark time. When I got out of the hospital he connected me with an AA group. I wasn't an everyday drunk, but I was using alcohol to cope with my feelings. The drinking contributed to my affair and pornography consumption. My pastor thought AA would help, and he was right. It gave me the discipline, structure and support to break the isolation and denial so I could begin to rebuild my life.

I also started to attend a men's group at my church. These men shared their struggles to live the life that God calls us to do. My feelings of isolation and self-pity broke down seeing other men struggling with sin but becoming stronger in faith and solidarity. I began to connect with these men who were really trying to live a life of virtue and faithfulness.

In one of our meetings, I shared about the abortion. It turned out that a couple of the men had also participated in an abortion in their past, so we went through a post-abortion Bible-study program together with our pastor. It was very painful to face my role in the abortion decision – how I manipulated Betsy to accept my "rational" reasons to participate in the death of our first child.

The truth is I sacrificed my first-born son on the altar of perfectionism and pride. Facing this reality was excruciating, but absolutely essential to my healing. Ultimately, it was the key to my liberation. I stopped trying to be perfect and have the perfect life, but threw myself at the foot of the Cross and acknowledged my inner poverty and sinfulness and my desperate need for a Savior. Jesus picked me up out of the mud, cleansed me in the blood and water flowing from His side, and restored my dignity and self worth. I looked at how my childhood led to the development of this deadly perfectionism. The other men and I named our children together and honored their short time on this earth. We shared the hope of seeing them again in heaven, God willing. I named my son David.

I am so grateful that my pastor and his wife reflected the love of Jesus to me at a time when I thought death was the only answer to my pain. I remarried a wonderful woman I met at my church, and we have two great kids, a son and daughter. My son John, from my first marriage, is in college now. I have tried to share with him through the years the lessons that I learned in life, especially those taught to me from my brothers in faith.

They taught me that being a man was not about being perfect, having a perfect past, or having the perfect life, home, job or car. Being a man is more about loving and protecting the people God places in our care. If we trust God and live according to His will as revealed in His Word, He will make up for what is lacking in us, and give us the support of other people to help us on our journey. God wants us to be faithful more than He wants us to be perfect. I pray that my son John will build upon this foundation of faith in his own life, and while every life has its pain and challenges, I pray each day that God will bless him, and all my children, with His peace and protect them from all evil.

My new job requires a long commute and I have to leave for work early each day. I try to make some time before I leave the house to pray, often as the first rays of light begin to shine over the horizon and the house is quiet and still. Many days as the warmth of the sun fills our family room, I find myself reflecting on the promise of a new day and the hope of resurrection and eternal life. Along side this joy I sometimes feel sadness and miss my son, David. But I also have been given the special gift in prayer that I want to share with any of you who are grieving the loss of your child to abortion. God has allowed me to see a glimpse of an awesome truth.

One day when my life is ended, I will see the face of my aborted son, David, for the very first time. We will embrace with joy, dancing in the presence of the Lord as the Israelite King danced before the Ark of the Covenant and we will be together for all eternity, joyfully praising our Creator:

> *And David, wearing a linen apron, came dancing before the Lord with abandon as he and all the Israelites were bringing up the ark of the Lord with shouts of joy and to the sound of the horn. (2 Samuel, chapter 6, 14-15)*

Chapter Three
I Married A Post Abortive Woman

By James McNeil

I married a post-abortive woman with the naive notion that if I loved her enough and accepted her unconditionally, the effect her two abortions had on her would somehow work itself out. Time may heal some wounds, but I can tell you now from experience, an abortion wound is not one of them.

Like Kathleen, your wife may not even be willing to admit that she is struggling with a past abortion. For some women, outward signs of pain, grief, loss and self-condemnation take years to appear because the abortion wound is repressed and tucked away deep down in their hearts.

Public discussion of abortion almost exclusively focuses on abortion's legality, which only reinforces the idea that abortion is strictly an ideological issue and not the intensely personal one that it is. Women who want to explore how an abortion has affected them emotionally and spiritually, until recently, have been given few options.

By the time Kathleen and I went through marriage preparations, we had already been sexually active for years. Kathleen was on the pill because she was scared of getting pregnant again, and this was fine with me. We had completely bought into the cultural lie that sexual activity is something adults should be able to take part in purely for gratification. My Catholic faith at the time was the surface type, a cultural Catholicism left over from being brought up in the Church, but not an intentional, adult faith. God was very patient with us.

At our Pre-Cana meetings with our priest, we played the part of the ideal, young couple preparing to get married. "Oh, yes, Father, of course we are open to having children," we said, and I think we both meant it in a vague, unexamined way. We got married and for a couple of years things seemed fine.

Inevitably, the subject of children came up, and the conversation never seemed to go very far. But since I was okay with not having children right away, the subject was easy enough to avoid. In time we had to face it. Her parents dropped hints at first, and then became more blunt in their attempts to encourage us to have children.

When I would bring up the idea of having children, Kathleen would say things like, "I don't deserve to be a mother." It started to dawn on me that unresolved pain, shame and grief related to her abortions were at the heart of her reluctance to have children. It was difficult to know how to address what was clearly a painful and sensitive wound in a way that would be helpful.

One time I said, "You can't sweep your abortions under the rug forever."

She said, "If I didn't sweep them under the rug, I couldn't live with myself." Kathleen had stuffed the pain and hurt deep down inside herself in order to cope, but in doing so she had walled off an area of her heart that could've otherwise been used to love herself and me. The price of avoiding the issue was taking a terrible toll on Kathleen and our marriage.

As the years passed, she was increasingly unable to completely squelch the emotions that came from her post-abortion pain and grief. She would occasionally freak out, scream at the top of her lungs, throw things, and break things. She told me she fantasized about cutting herself, and burning herself. I felt so powerless and confused, and I had no idea how to help her, except to calm and soothe her in the moment. I was unable by myself to help her face her abortions and embrace a future that included having children. No matter the tactics, or entry point to the discussion, we wound up at odds, and back at square one when it was over. It was like banging our heads against a brick wall.

One of the hardest things to live with was the fact that our relationship itself was held up as proof that the abortions had been the right thing to do. Kathleen would say to me, "I can't imagine my life without you, and if I had had the two children, I wouldn't have you, so the abortions must have been the right thing to do." What do you say in response to a statement like that? To have our love serve as justification for her abortions hurt deeply, and I felt powerless to do anything to help her or us.

When Kathleen became pregnant the first time, at age 18, she worried about her parents being ashamed of her. That, coupled with the thought that a baby would derail her plans to be successful in school, weighed heavily in her decision to have an abortion. Another abortion followed a year later. She continued to justify her abortions to herself by excelling in school. She took on an ambitious schedule – 21 hours of classes while working as the head of a women's residence hall floor – and earned a 4.0. To all eyes, she was the model student and the perfect daughter. The demanding schedule served two purposes: it made the deal she made with herself seem worth it, and it kept her so occupied that she was able to keep her emotions around the abortion buried. However, this came with a price. Over time she became detached and unemotional. Sequestering that wounded part of her heart meant walling off areas of caring, emotion and love.

A husband who is not the father of the aborted child faces an additional hurdle to clear before he can even start to discuss the abortion with his wife. A post-abortive man can say to his wife, "We both have a share in this. Let's face our abortion together." If you're not the father, though, you may get some very defensive responses as you introduce this very sensitive subject:

"You weren't involved, so you could never understand."

"What right do you have to judge me?"

"Oh that's right, I forgot. You're perfect. You've never done anything wrong."

"This doesn't involve you, so please drop it. I'll handle this on my own."

These defensive and often angry responses serve as a shield to hide the deeper feelings of shame, unresolved grief, and self-loathing that often lie beneath the surface. Kathleen's way of "handling" this pain was to try to ignore it. I knew I wanted to have children eventually, and I saw the conflict with her unresolved abortion pain. The future, however, seemed far off. I was about to find out just how directly Kathleen's abortions could affect our marriage.

I was in a touring band for years, which was the main reason I had supported the idea of contraception – having children would derail the band's chance at success. Two years into our marriage, while I was on tour with the band, Kathleen began an affair with another man. The affair continued the following summer when I was again on tour.

I had been growing increasingly suspicious and finally stopped ducking the issue and asked her directly if she was having an affair. When she admitted it, I felt completely betrayed, undone, stabbed in the heart. I never, ever, thought it could happen to us. I thought we were bulletproof. For the better part of an hour, the conversation was heated. I had to know every excruciating detail of exactly how wrong things had gone.

And I asked the inevitable question, "Why?"

After we'd calmed down a bit, I said plainly, "One of two things is going to happen. We're either going to come together like never before and really put this back together, or we can get our marriage annulled." For a few days it was an open question, and, if not for the grace of God, we easily could have gone our separate ways.

In time I was able to see the connection between the abortions and the affair. To Kathleen, I represented having a family and facing her abortions, whereas the other man represented a return to the noncommittal good times we had shared in our dating years. In the moment of discovery, it's not much consolation, but in understanding your wife and the lengths to which she will go to avoid facing how her abortion has affected her, it does have value.

I learned later on that affairs, promiscuity, and sexual dysfunction are not uncommon for post-abortive women and men, who often sabotage their marriages to punish themselves.

The deepest desires of our heart for intimacy, pleasure and love are linked to the sexual component of our marital relationships. So it makes sense that symptoms of unresolved abortion pain can negatively affect our relationships.

Instead of separation and divorce, we went on a Marriage Encounter weekend retreat. When we repeated our vows to each other during the retreat, they meant more to us than ever before, and we rededicated ourselves to each other. The abortions did come up at the retreat, but again, the conversation went nowhere. But given all that had happened, both of us were relieved to escape with our marriage intact. The issue of the abortions would have to wait for another day. We were, however, already operating from a new strength.

About a year after the Marriage Encounter retreat, Kathleen was experiencing some serious depression she could not explain. Her violent screaming and destructive outbursts were as common as ever. She started seeing a psychiatrist, but visit after visit seemed to go nowhere. First-born children like Kathleen tend to want to please authority figures. Kathleen gave her therapist the "right" answers, but never the ones that revealed much. It is worth noting that many therapists on both sides of the abortion issue are ill equipped to treat post-abortive women and men. Many psychiatrists – like the rest of society – do not even recognize post-abortion trauma or grief. Even counselors who are willing to recognize abortion-related symptoms often lack the knowledge and resources to offer practical, effective treatment of this trauma.

Out of desperation, Kathleen's therapist asked to have me join them for a session. When she asked me what I thought was at the root of Kathleen's depression and acting out, I recounted all the things she had said to me over the years. All the "under a rug" and "I don't deserve to be a mother" comments came out. When I finished speaking I looked at Kathleen. She looked dumbfounded, like her deepest, darkest secret had been told.

It had.

I knew there were post-abortion-related websites out there and mentioned this to the psychiatrist. She said, "You both have a homework assignment. I want you to both go home and read up on what post-abortion resources are on the web."

I scoured the web for resources, and I hoped Kathleen was doing the same thing. I found Rachel's Vineyard (www.rachelsvineyard.com). I read almost everything the site had to say about their healing weekend retreats, and started looking at available cities and dates.

There was no retreat in our city at that time (1999) and the nearest was a 10- to 15-hour drive. The closest – in location and date – was in Kansas City. For days I sat on this information, all the while looking for the right way to start a conversation about what we'd been learning through our web searches. One night, Kathleen was already in bed and I was nearby checking my e-mail.

She said, "Sweetheart, how far is it to Kansas City?"

Surprised, I said, "It's about an 11-hour drive, why?" We had both been sizing up the same Rachel's Vineyard retreat. We just looked at each other and smiled. We knew then that God had been guiding our web searches.

I had been e-mailing back and forth with Theresa Burke, the executive director of Rachel's Vineyard. She encouraged me to go on the retreat with Kathleen. Once Kathleen had decided to go, she resisted the idea of me coming along. She insisted that, since I was not involved in the pregnancies, she would go alone. I told her that a leader from Rachel's Vineyard had advised me to accompany her. She relented and we started making travel plans.

Once we got to Kansas City, we stopped at a restaurant for dinner before the retreat. Kathleen said, "If you weren't here with me, I'd turn right around and drive back home."

I held her hand, looked into her eyes, and told her, "I love you, and this is going to be a very good thing for us both."

To explain the Rachel's Vineyard retreat here would require at least a chapter of its own, if not its own book. Suffice it to say that the retreat's guided scripture mediations and exercises, group sharing, and naming of Kathleen's children, while not easy to go through, were very healing for us. Kathleen read a letter to her children at the memorial service at the end of the weekend, and I spiritually adopted her two children. So many tears were shed that weekend, but at the end there was joy – great joy – peace and restoration, for us and for the others on the retreat.

I have never been more convinced that God moves powerfully to love his wounded people back to life, than that weekend in Kansas City. I saw, first-hand, the Holy Spirit act through the human compassion, sensitivity and skill of that wonderful retreat team of lay people, professionals and clergy. It was a mountaintop experience for Kathleen and me. We emerged renewed. The trip home from Kansas City felt like the exhilarating road trips we'd enjoyed years before. We were floating on air from the experience.

Kathleen's abortion wound was like a cancer. The retreat had removed the cancer, but there was still much healing to be done in our marriage. There is no overnight solution to the problems abortion causes, and if you are struggling to find a way to help your wife find healing, take heart and trust that the slow process is worth your time and effort.

Kathleen was still not ready to become a mother, and still questioned whether she could bear a child. I assured her she could, but we remained at an impasse for another few years. I heard about the health risks associated with the pill, and started to question the morality of it as well. I knew the Catholic Church had a teaching against contraception, but until then, I had sided with the larger culture, which considers the Church to be a repressive organization, out of step with the times. I picked up a copy of *Humanae Vitae*, and read it cover to cover. The logic made sense to me. I saw clearly why the Church was right to teach that the use of artificial birth control was sinful and harmful.

I told Kathleen about my change of heart and she seemed very skeptical. I did not draw a line in the sand at first, but ultimately, I had to. I could no longer, in good conscience, have sex and use artificial birth control. I suggested we look into Natural Family Planning (NFP), which is a method of charting your fertility signs to know exactly when you are fertile and when you are not. The Church approves of NFP because sexual activity is open to children, and because only natural means are used to postpone having children. She resisted at first, but eventually she agreed to go to an NFP class through our diocese.

Kathleen got off the pill and it took several months for her fertility to even out. Once it did, and once we got comfortable with how NFP worked, we both liked it. We felt good about her better health. We grew more and more confident that it was effective. Over time, it produced closeness impossible with artificial birth control. The amount of restraint you have to exercise to avoid pregnancy is a small price to pay for the added intimacy and closer friendship that comes from working selflessly toward a desired end. Natural Family Planning was another step in God's healing work in our marriage.

The last step was making love on a night we knew Kathleen was fertile. Knowing that and intentionally deciding to go ahead was to participate in a love deeper than I could imagine. Several weeks later, we got confirmation – Kathleen was pregnant. The birth of our daughter was the final step in Kathleen's healing. Kathleen told me later on that she had prayed for intercession from her children in heaven, for her pregnancy to be healthy and without complications.

We went though Bradley Natural Childbirth classes, which taught us a team approach in which I learned how to relax and sooth Kathleen and how to be her labor coach on the big day. We read every book we could get our hands on, did our nightly exercises and massage routine, and Kathleen tried to eat all the right foods. Kathleen labored for six hours before giving birth to our daughter naturally and without complications. Our daughter is the most beautiful and wonderful gift God has ever given us.

When I look at our past and the steps we had to take to deal with the confusion and frustration abortion caused in our lives, I know that each step was important and could not be rushed. God is so patient. God is so faithful, and God works miracles when we stay humble and open to him acting in our lives. Sometimes that requires hard work on our part. Your wife and your marriage is worth that hard work and I would just encourage you to stay at it.

The steps we took toward healing may not be exactly the same steps you and your wife will take, or they may come in a different order, so don't read this as a simple "to do" list. Hopefully, reading about our experience of healing will give you tools to use along your healing journey. Here are a few final tips:

- Be lovingly persistent with your wife. To the degree possible, frame everything you say in the context of how the two of you can approach healing together. If she lashes out at you in anger and tells you it's not your concern, again, love your wife enough to let the hurtful words bounce off of you. She does not mean it. Ask God to give you the strength, the right words to say, or the sense to just turn out the lights, rub her back, tell her you love her and let her fall asleep in your arms. Tomorrow will provide another opportunity.
- Stay open to what God wants you to learn through each experience. Be prepared to listen when your wife is ready to talk. Be understanding and keep a sense of humor. Sometimes a good laugh can remind you both what great friends you are right when you need to be

reminded and also provide a welcome emotional break from the hard work you've completed and what lies ahead. Laughing together, or crying together for that matter, can be very healing and unifying. An abortion wound is a wedge between you, so every step you can take toward being a team is a step toward healing.

- For a better understanding of how abortion affects women, read *Forbidden Grief: the Unspoken Pain of Abortion*, by Rachel's Vineyard founder Dr. Theresa Burke (available at www.rachelsvineyard.org under "publications" or by calling 1 877 HOPE 4 ME). I found it to be very helpful in understanding my wife's post-abortive symptoms and behavior. A man can never understand the depths of how an abortion affects a woman, but we owe it to the women we love to learn as much as we can about the possible manifestations of post-abortion syndrome.

- God's love, forgiveness and mercy are the only things that can truly heal a heart broken by abortion. If your wife is openly looking for a way to face her abortion experience and move through it in a positive way, I cannot recommend strongly enough that you find a Rachel's Vineyard retreat in your area and attend as a couple. Visit www.rachelsvineyard.org, or call 1 877 HOPE 4 ME (1 877 467 3463). Retreats are open to all people – women, men, grandparents and siblings of aborted children – regardless of one's faith tradition or background. Rachel's Vineyard is a ministry of Priests For Life.

- Consider attending one of these weekend programs for strengthening your marriage: 1. Marriage Encounter - www.wwme.org/new.html or 1 800 795-5683. 2. Retrouvaille - www.retrouvaille.org or 1 800-470-2230. You can attend these programs before or after your Rachel's Vineyard retreat and both will work to complement the healing work of Rachel's Vineyard.

- Talk to a priest, pastor, counselor, or friend who understands the struggles and symptoms of post abortion pain. More and more, clergy and other counselors are being trained in how to help people work through post-abortion issues.
- Stay at it. Pray. Pray some more, and let love underpin your every word and action.

Chapter Four
My Abortion Story: A Father's Perspective

By Jason Baier

In loving memory of my son, Jamie.

Abortion was one of those things I thought would never touch my life. In fact, I really didn't even have an opinion about it. I had heard about the medical "breakthroughs" that were being made with the use of fetal tissue, so it didn't seem like such a bad thing. But it came as a big surprise when I had to face the issue personally. First, I was surprised by my response to it, and second, at the profound impact an abortion would have on my life.

I had a happy childhood growing up in the Pennsylvania countryside, and although I didn't have many friends to play with, I did have two younger brothers to pal around with. We enjoyed outdoor activities like camping, fishing and swimming. In school, I pretty much kept to myself. I was voted shiest in my graduating class. I was never good at sports, but was most comfortable performing on stage. But my true passion was the armed forces. I was actively involved in the Civil Air Patrol and signed up for the Air Force when I was a junior in high school.

I left for boot camp right after finishing high school in 1989. I loved the physical and mental challenges. I worked hard and graduated with honors. I volunteered as a student leader during my technical training and couldn't wait to get to my permanent assignment. My military career was off to a great start.

My permanent station was at Andrews Air Force Base in Washington D.C. I quickly made new friends and discovered the joys of partying. All through high school I never even had a single drink, so I broke loose and partied hard. One night I met a girl and had my first sexual encounter. We ended up dating for a couple years.

During Desert Storm, many of my friends went to Kuwait. My girlfriend also broke up with me for some other guy, which crushed my self-esteem. Life got boring, so I spent a lot of my time just sitting around drinking. I also became promiscuous and would sleep with anyone that would show interest. I started oversleeping a lot and got into trouble for being late for work. I no longer enjoyed my job, and I had lost myself in alcohol and sexual addiction.

I left the Air Force in 1993, returned to my home town and got a job in retail. I soon ran into Andrea, a childhood friend whom I hadn't seen in years. She had just moved back from New York and had a five-month-old daughter named Kelly. Andrea and I started hanging out together and our relationship quickly became sexual. I bonded well with Kelly and before long, we decided to get an apartment together.

It didn't take long for me to realize I enjoyed family life, so I asked Andrea to marry me, and she agreed. We didn't make much money, but I worked hard to support Andrea and Kelly and was getting frequent promotions at work. Then one day I came home from work and Andrea told me she was pregnant. I was thrilled! Kelly was almost three years old and now she'd have a baby brother or sister. I told everyone in my family and at work that I was going to be a daddy.

At first, Andrea seemed happy about the pregnancy. But after a few weeks, things started to change. She was saying things like, "I'm not sure if we're ready for another child," and, "We can't afford to have a baby right now." I tried to assure her that we'd be fine. I offered to get a second job so I could better support her and the kids. But her doubts and fears increased and finally she told me she was considering abortion. Suddenly, I was terrified. I had never given much thought about abortion and hadn't even considered the possibility of aborting our own child. For me, that just wasn't an option. I was excited about being a father and didn't want to lose this child.

Our discussions turned into arguments. Our arguments turned into fights. It was impossible to have a civilized conversation about it. We were on opposite ends of the spectrum. Every time I tried to plead with her to keep our child, she would tell me it wasn't my decision… that it was her body and her choice. I even offered that if she just had the baby, then I would raise it on my own. I became so desperate that I went to a lawyer to see if I could stop her. Unfortunately, he told me there was no legal action I could take. As a father, I had no rights until the child was born. I thought it was ironic that a man could go to jail for not paying child support, but could do nothing to protect his unborn child. The only hope I had was that Andrea couldn't afford to get an abortion and I wasn't about to pay for it.

It was on February 25th, 1995 that my life changed forever. Andrea had gone to the clinic and had the abortion while I was at work. Her sister, Cathy, had paid for the procedure and was the one who told me that it was done. The last thing I remember after hearing the news was lying in the parking lot of a bar screaming at the top of my lungs. I have no recollection of how I got home or how many days passed before I moved back in with my parents.

The next several months were just a blur. Andrea and I didn't talk for a long time, and when we did, the conversations were heated. But somehow we worked things out and I moved back in with her. But things would never be the same. I started having anger issues, had trouble staying focused on my job, and would often break down and cry from depression. Andrea also seemed depressed at times and started exhibiting reckless behaviors. Eventually our relationship collapsed and she moved out.

My depression was getting worse and I was angry all the time at everything and everyone. I was drinking heavily and started using drugs. I was also having trouble sleeping at night and my job performance began to suffer. I was stricken with panic attacks that seemed to come for no reason and without warning. I decided to see a psychiatrist before I lost all control. He identified the fact that my problems stemmed from the abortion, diagnosed me with severe depression and border-line psychosis, and prescribed medications for depression, anxiety and sleeplessness. At his recommendation, I also took a three-month leave of absence from work and entered a hospital treatment program.

All the medications seemed to just cloud my head instead of making me feel better, so I continued using illegal drugs and alcohol on top of the medications. In the hospital, I was surrounded by people with severe emotional problems all day long, which didn't seem to help. During my counseling sessions and group therapies, we talked about my emotions and how to control them, but never targeted the source of my problems… the abortion. No one seemed to understand or know how to help me deal with my loss. Since I wasn't working, I was quickly running out of money. I pawned everything I owned just to buy my medications and support my drug habits. I also found myself in and out of meaningless relationships.

Finally, I reached a point where I felt there was no hope. I figured no one would ever understand, that I must be crazy for even feeling a sense of loss, and that I would never get better. Life was no longer worth living. So I sat at my dining room table with the last bottle of sleeping pills I had. "This will be easy" I thought to myself. I would just swallow all these pills, lay down, fall asleep and never wake up.

I poured the pills into my hand and as I raised them to put them in my mouth, I was suddenly overcome by a feeling of intense warmth over my entire body and complete peace. My mouth was open and my hand was only a few inches away, yet there I sat, frozen, staring at the wall. All of a sudden, with an earthquake-like shudder, the pills flew out of my hand and I collapsed to the floor sobbing like a child. For the next 45 minutes or so, I laid there on the floor crying, trying to figure out what had just happened. Then, in a moment, I felt compelled to grab the phone book. I didn't know what I was looking for, but I flipped it open and right there on the first page I came to was an ad with large print asking if I was "Looking for a new home?" It was an ad for a church.

We never went to church while I was growing up. When I was younger, I had believed in God, but the older I got, the less faith I had. At this point of my life, I actually considered myself to be an atheist. I asked myself, "How could there be a loving God with this world as messed up as it is?" I used all the problems in my life to rationalize that we were alone in this world. But it was at this lowest moment in my life that I realized I had been wrong. To this day I believe God reached down and comforted me at a time when I needed Him most, even though I wasn't looking for Him. It reminds me of the *Footprints in the Sand* poem.

So, I called the church and made an appointment to meet with the pastor. When we met, I told him my story and, for the first time, he was someone who understood my loss and the pain I was going through. He also identified that I exhibited codependent behaviors with my drug and alcohol addictions and my reckless relationships. He put me in touch with a codependency 12-step support group and encouraged me to start attending church services. So began my path to healing and my journey in faith.

I started going to church services every Sunday and absorbed everything I could about God's love, mercy and grace. I also worked very hard at completing my 12 steps. I didn't like the way the medications made me feel, so without my psychiatrist's permission, I took myself off the meds. I also quit using drugs and was able to cut back my drinking to a responsible level. I came across a book in the bookstore called *Men and Abortion: A Path to Healing* by Dr. Catherine Coyle. Here was someone who knew exactly what I had been through and I discovered that I wasn't alone. There were other men, just like me, who had walked this path before, which was very helpful to my healing. I got a new job and was earning an income again. I also started volunteering at a crisis pregnancy center just doing odds-and-end type jobs. My new hobby was country line dancing, and that is how I met Nancy, the woman who would become my wife.

As time went by and I put my life back together, the focus on healing from my abortion experience was put on the back burner. Nancy and I moved to Phoenix to start over, hoping to forget about my past problems altogether. I got a good job making more money than ever before, but it meant working a lot of hours. We found a church where we got married a year later, but eventually stopped attending because I was working almost every weekend. Overall, I thought life was good, but some problems began to surface.

I started feeling depressed again, my anxiety level was high, I was tired all the time, and I would get angry over the smallest things. I also noticed that February was always a difficult month for me, as it was the anniversary of the abortion. I didn't want to deal with my abortion experience anymore, so I denied the truth; I hadn't finished healing from it. I was just too busy to bother. All I cared about was working harder, hoping to keep myself occupied.

Then, just as my life had changed before, it was about to change again. My wife and I decided to go see a movie, which we didn't do very often. The movie we saw was *The Passion of the Christ.* Who would have thought a movie could be so powerful and draw so much emotion? Sure I knew the story of how Christ gave his life for us, but to actually see it portrayed so realistically… well, words can't describe it. We left the theatre in complete silence and the next week was an emotional rollercoaster for me. I came to realize how much I needed Christ in my life and that I had to finish my healing. So we found a new church, I gave my life to Christ, was baptized, and started focusing on any unresolved issues I still had.

It was on the 10th anniversary of the abortion that I sensed a calling to begin ministering to others. I felt I had fully healed, so I answered that calling by creating the organization Fatherhood Forever Foundation. I wanted other men to find the help and understanding they need much easier than it was for me, so I began collecting resources from across the country that work with men and created the Men's Healing Network. As I promoted the organization, I found myself meeting many wonderful people working in pro-life ministry and post-abortion healing services.

Two of those people I met were Rachel's Vineyard weekend retreat counselors who encouraged me to attend a retreat for the experience. I agreed to go because I saw it as a chance to explore one of the organizations listed in the Men's Healing Network and to see if it was something I would be interested in helping with. Little did I realize what I was really getting myself into!

When I arrived at the retreat, I put on a big smile and acted as though I had no concerns about what would happen during the weekend. I'll admit I was a bit nervous, but couldn't put my finger on the reason why. I was relieved to discover I wasn't the only guy that would be attending. The retreat location was absolutely beautiful and I was soon at ease with the whole idea of spending the weekend there. That is until the retreat officially started.

Within minutes of starting, I found myself putting up barriers. I became stone-faced and sat with my arms crossed in defiance; attempting to resist any emotion the staff might be trying to pull from me. "I'm already healed", I thought to myself. "There's nothing they can do or say to make me think otherwise." My pride got the best of me and I felt compelled to express my "discomfort" with one of the staff members during a break. Her simple words of comfort and understanding quickly put me at ease. When I went to bed that night, I told myself that although I was going to be strong, I would at least be more open tomorrow.

And then tomorrow arrived, and I was not so strong. I came to realize that I still had a great deal of unresolved anger toward the mother of my child, who I thought I had forgiven, and guilt for not being able to prevent the abortion. But my emotional breaking point was when I discovered I still had sorrow and despair buried deep within my heart. I hadn't cried that hard since the day I lost my child. I cried not only for the loss of my child, but for having fooled myself into believing I was healed. I was angry and ashamed with myself.

It was at my lowest point of the weekend that nothing short of a miracle occurred. I was suddenly overcome with a sense of peace that I had only experienced once before in my life. I embraced these emotions and let all my pain and anger go. For the first time ever, I was able to see clearly and know that I had reason to be joyful again. I was able to put to rest all those thoughts and feelings that were holding me back from being the person I was meant to be. My eyes were fully opened.

Since the retreat, I've had new revelations and convictions that have paved the way for a brighter future. I've discovered truths I had been blind to in the past, which have raised me up in faith and hope. I no longer mourn the loss of my son, to whom I gave the name Jamie, but rather I rejoice in what I have gained… a deeper relationship with Christ and my son, and knowledge of the truth that one day I will be reunited with them in eternity.

Chapter Five
Respecting Rachel

She must be the daughter of one of the organizers, I thought. So young. But upset. Crying recently. Sitting in a chair next to others who were obviously guests at the retreat. Daughter of one of them? Sorry because of an abortion by her mother?

No, she was a guest like the rest of us, there for herself. Maybe just looked so young because I'm not so young.

But later she told her story and she was nearly as young as she looked; just turned fifteen; had an abortion at age 14. Unmarried-no job-freshman in high school.

She was surprised when she found herself pregnant, but she knew she wanted the baby. "I'll protect you," she had told the unborn child.

But her boyfriend insisted on the abortion. His mother thought it was the best thing. Her own mother supported it. Who wanted her to have it? Should she be selfish, and do what only she wanted? How would she provide for herself and the child? Life would be so hard!

So she had the abortion. And descended into despair. She was inconsolable. Wanted only one thing: her baby back. But no one could give it to her.

She knew others had pushed her to have the abortion but She was not blaming others. Her emotion was grief, the sense of permanent loss. Wanting what cannot be had. When she did any blaming, she blamed herself.

I came to this Rachel's Vineyard retreat at the request of my wife. Because she had an abortion. Or at least that's how I thought of it.

She had one under circumstances far less taxing than the fourteen year-old faced. At that time she already had children, a house and a husband with a decent income. No one pushing her to have the abortion. But she alone decided to have it. At least that's how I thought of it.

I was that husband.

My wife had a great deal of difficulty over the abortion in the years after. What to me were sporadic, unexplainable bad times. Watching our children play, and being saddened instead of cheered. Watching old home videos of our infants and having to leave the room. Driven to take on challenging projects outside of the home and away from the family.

It seemed like rejection at times, and even of the children. It hurt, but it was mysterious and risky, and I did not question or challenge. She always had independence and a defiance of restraints of her pursuits; that came with the package, I thought. So I let it go… or tried to.

Then we began drifting from our agnostic past. Toward Christianity. Though I didn't know it, she decided she was burdened by the abortion, and had been trying to run from it, mentally at least. Then she discovered something for people burdened about past abortion--Rachel's Vineyard retreats. She went to one alone for a weekend, and came back bright and bouncy. Enthusiastic about the retreat. Relieved. No anger at anyone; as if a cloud had lifted. She told me some stories about others there; not too much about her own experience. It was puzzling to me why these women were so burdened by abortions, often long past, especially when they were often in circumstances where a pregnancy was an overwhelming burden.

She remained engaged with the people she met at Rachel's Vineyard and a few months later asked me to attend a retreat. It was easy to agree. It would be some months away; it was just a weekend. And I would learn what she was talking about and be able to sympathize more with her.

I cannot say that I looked forward to the retreat. I can say that time flew by quickly in the months before and I almost never thought about it. Until it was a week away. Then I began to wish it were still a month away. To wish I had the weekend free. Then on the drive there my concerns were less about what I could be doing and more about what I might face. It could be difficult. No football to watch. Not sure if other men would be there. Just women having a tough time in life. Could they help me? Not likely, I thought. But it would all be over in a weekend.

We met people Friday evening, and then went around the room telling why we were there. Each woman had a very different, but very hard story. One unmarried mother raising an eleven year old, the only bright spot in her life, and sadly, then angrily missing her three aborted children. Another woman, happily married, or at least happy with her marriage and her children. But missing one, conceived on a one-night stand in college with a man she never married. But haunted, guilty about her good life, her seemingly perfect family, feeling undeserving because she had abandoned that first, never-born child.

A twenty-four year old...twice guilty. Already burdened by an abortion as an unwed 21-year-old, she told this scorching story about herself: Her best friend conceived a child several months after her abortion. She was consumed with quiet envy and ran a campaign to get her friend to abort her unborn child. She was successful. Her friend was unhappy. She was driven by guilt to confess to her friend, who was her best friend no more. No judge could have pronounced a more severe conclusion about these actions than this distraught young woman; she was sad on her good days, depressed on the rest, and suicidal on the worst.

Then there was a smart, attractive woman who spoke calmly of her own abortion. Circumstances entirely different from the others. She was the only one who was married when she had the abortion. She already had other healthy children. Husband with a good job. They were even pro-life Catholics. But the pregnancy was unplanned. Inconvenient. For her husband, that made it unwanted. She was uncomfortable. But not firm in opposing his wishes. She had the abortion.

Now her grief was unplanned. Her sadness inconvenient. Her anger at her husband unwanted by both, and a heap more inconvenient to him than another child might have been.

She recognized that she was different from the others, because her pregnancy did not create overwhelming problems. Just a situation she had faced successfully before.

Like my wife.

The stories had all been riveting. Every one, every word. So far outside of the normal, practiced methods of human communication, where the speaker wants to create a certain impression or effect in the listener. Not here. These women bared their souls. They spoke with too much humility, too much knowledge, and too little mercy. Relentless! No excuses, no rationalizations.

I admired the unvarnished verdicts; the moral clarity with which the women spoke. They knew. They knew they had committed a fundamental offense against themselves, their very nature. And if God did not approve of their abortions, so much the better for Him. They agreed with Him. Religion was not why they thought their abortions wrong. They held to their religious beliefs because those beliefs supported what they knew, from direct and painful personal insight, about life unborn, and their lives as potential mothers. They just knew, and no solid argument, much less a slick rationalization, would relieve them of their heavy knowledge. They knew.

I saw myself in a very different position from them. I had not been suffering from overwhelming guilt. After all, I had not had an abortion. So what did I have to be guilty about?

As I listened, I occasionally thought of these women, "Don't you know about denial? It has its uses."

I thought about how tough it would be to work and hold the family together while suffering as they did. It would not be possible. A responsible man could not do it. He would have to get over, or bury, or just deny the problem. Yes, he would.

When my turn came, I made clear that I was in a very different position from them. Never had an abortion. I mean, never even made anyone have an abortion. My wife had one. That's all. Well I guess we had one, you could say. And I told them I admired their searing honesty. And told them that they had all faced circumstances much more challenging than we had, yes, it was "we" now. Except for the one woman who had an abortion while married, who nodded knowingly and agreed heartily that we were two apart, two without excuses worth airing after hearing of the traumatic plights of our fellow-sufferers. We seemed to be thinking the same thing. We seemed to be suffering less. But we were surely guiltier than any of these others. If they really had a choice, what did we have? Each of them, in our circumstances, would have had the child without hesitation.

What was wrong with us?

That's not what I was asking. It was "What's wrong with me?"

What rationalizations have I absorbed from this indulgent society to allow me to let myself off the hook for what I have done, and what I have failed to do?

It was a long and difficult night. The denial fell away in the light of the moral clarity shown by all of the women there.

I dropped my own self-serving protections, and examined my own role in the abortion with the self-critical perspective these women showed.

I was guilty of abortion! There was no getting around it. Ghastly!

I had put my wife through that. Then let her suffer those years without insight or sympathy. Doubly guilty!

What I had done was raise no objection to the idea of abortion. Drove her to the clinic. Paid cash. Watched without question or objection. Never discussed it, before or after.

I had not created the right context for a surprise pregnancy. I had not created the right welcoming home before the pregnancy ever happened. It simply should not have been a matter up for debate after the fact, at a potentially difficult time. But when that did happen, I should have spoken, and led us in the right direction.

I now faced what I had done. I had chosen my own short-run convenience ahead of anything else. I chose what I thought was the easier road. And then I buried that choice. Or so I thought.

After that Friday night, I was no longer the one guest who had not had an abortion. I was fully engaged, like the others, and working through the program for myself. The women continued to impress with their honesty; I tried to repay them with honesty about myself. The early part of the retreat had been such an eye-opener to me that I decided to follow with rigor the remainder of the program. Parts were a great challenge. But I stuck with it, and was rewarded by the results.

I left the retreat on Sunday extremely eager to see my wife, to tell her how sorry I was, to let her know that I now had some insight into what she had been through.

And I knew, too, that issues I had with her, resentments about this and that over the years, were gone. Lifted, because my offense here was greater than all of hers squared. The scale was not the same. It was not as though I proposed some trade in my favor, I just was not interested in her past offenses any more. They did not matter. I saw her in a fresh light, as someone who had overcome a great deal, by her own inner strength. Who had pushed and probed about her pain, though it took her down the hard road to painful truth.

After all, isn't the easy road after abortion to accept the pro-choice arguments? To decide that it's a blob of tissue, a private decision, nobody's business but yours? Doesn't every selfish motive drive one in that direction?

Maybe. But not every motive is selfish. And not everyone is attracted to selfish rationalization when the going gets tough. My wife was one of the strong ones, and I am eternally grateful for that. And grateful that she showed me the short cut after her long search for healing after abortion. For after painful truth is the possibility of lasting forgiveness, of your spouse and yourself. And renewed respect for the sacred lives that surround you.

Chapter Six
A Prison of Ice

The day of the abortion was a warm gray day, with a very fine mist falling from the sky. We drove silently to the abortion center, and parked in the lot. "Do you want me to come in with you?" I asked. She told me to wait in the car, and to be truthful, I was relieved not to go into that place.

As I was sitting there alone in my car it began to hit me what was about to happen. How can I sit here and let this happen to my baby—that's my son or daughter they are going to kill! I jumped out of the car and ran into the building. The receptionist told me that Janet was in the procedure room and that I could take a seat and wait. I blew past her and after bursting through a few doors came upon a scene that burned into my mind and haunted me for months after.

As I entered that room, Janet screamed out "John, what are you doing?"

The doctor looked at me and smiled, "John we are just finishing up, everything went fine." I looked at Janet; she was white as a ghost and crying. Our baby had just been killed! I was unable to stop it. I even paid for it to happen! It was a living nightmare. I stormed out of the building knocking over some chairs and a trashcan in my rage. We drove home in silence, both in shock.

I first met Janet in a softball league. She was actually a pretty good player and a great pitcher. We hit it off right away. We were very attracted to one another and after a lot of mutual flirting I finally got the nerve to ask her out. I knew she already had a child from a previous relationship, but I was so taken by her that didn't bother me a bit. Janet just started a new job as a para-legal secretary. She really wanted to get her life together so she could be a role model for her daughter who was four years old at the time. We progressed to regular dating and eventually we began to have sex. I was falling deeper in love with her and grew attached to her daughter as well.

When we had sex we would always use birth control. There was one night we went out together, we had a great time. We went to hear a local band, went dancing, and partied it up. When we go back to her apartment we just threw caution to the wind, and had unprotected sex. I am not sure why we did that, I think we were just caught up in the joy of being together, of the love and passion we shared.

A few weeks later she told me she missed her period. My first reaction was fear, but I also felt excited about being a dad. I was in love with Janet, and hoped we could work it out. Unfortunately Janet had a much different reaction.

Janet was already a single parent. She just started a new job she loved. She was embarrassed to be in this situation again, and felt that she couldn't face family and friends again with another unplanned pregnancy. Janet felt stupid, foolish and angry. I told her that I would help her, and that we could get married. She didn't want to marry because of the pregnancy, and I don't think she trusted that I would be there for her down the line (she had been down that road before).

That's when Janet first said it: "I want to get an abortion." I felt sick to my stomach. I felt like this is my kid too, and I wanted to have this baby. But I was also scared of losing Janet. Maybe Janet sensed my fear. Or maybe I wasn't strong enough in opposing it. Maybe it wouldn't have mattered. I don't know. I knew that she was set on getting that abortion.

I decided to support Janet in her in her decision, pay for the abortion and drive her to the abortion center.

In the days ahead after that nightmare in the abortion center, I was filled with rage at the abortion doctor and Janet. How could they do this to my child! Was this the only way? Why couldn't we work this out and save our baby! Why was this child sacrificed because of our stupidity! I stopped seeing Janet. I was too filled with rage, anger and grief to even look at her.

For the next four months after the abortion, I slept very little. I would lie awake at night and stare at the ceiling reliving that day. When I slept I would dream of that same horrible scene where I would break into the abortion procedure room. But in these nightmares, I would find my dead baby, in pieces. I would awaken from this terror filled with rage and grief—how could I let this happen, how could I have been so weak, so evil? But my grief quickly transformed into a seething rage at Janet, the abortionist, and the abortion business that took the life of my child. I was sure that I would never escape this nightmare-it was God's punishment for my sins.

I returned to work, and looking back now, the routine of work during those months saved my life. At least during the day I could stay focused on work and escape my private hell—but at night, the demons returned to torture me till dawn. I would get a few hours sleep if I was lucky, and just try to get through each day.

After four months of this hell a ray of light shown into my darkness. I continued to go to church off and on after the abortion. I would sit in the back like a zombie, waiting for the Lord to strike me with lightning—I was actually praying that he would take my life. I also prayed for the strength not to take my own life, or worse, do something stupid to the clinic or doctor and get arrested. But God gave me a road to travel that would save my life and much more.

This particular Sunday, near the close of the service, a speaker got up and talked to us about a healing weekend for people involved in abortion called Rachel's Vineyard Retreats. There were pamphlets in the back of the church and I took one. I read it and picked up the phone for days to make that call but couldn't bring myself to finish dialing that last number! Finally, I made the call and found that men were welcome, and registered for their next weekend retreat.

I can't say I was especially confident that this would help me. It was more like "If this doesn't help me, I don't really want to go on living. This is my last hope, the last stop." I arrived at the retreat house Friday evening after work. Like my father, I'm a man of few words and I am shy when I first meet people. I was in so much pain, so filled with anger at Janet, the doctor, and myself that I felt like I was trapped inside an invisible layer of ice that I couldn't get out of, and that I wouldn't let anyone enter into.

The retreat began and I very slowly started to thaw. On Saturday morning of the retreat we broke into groups to share the story of our abortion. There were a number of women in my group. Hearing their stories of what they went through emotionally in making the decision, and how they suffered after their abortion, began to lessen my rage at Janet. There were scripture meditations used throughout the retreat based on stories from the New Testament. These help us to personally enter into the story.

One of these meditations focuses on the story of the blind beggar who Jesus asks, "what do you want me to do for you." Wasn't it clear that the guy was blind and wanted to see Jesus! But I learned that Jesus required our "yes." He required our participation in his saving action. These exercises and meditations were powerful, and, even as scared and doubting as I was, I was meeting Jesus in those exercises while asking Him quietly to heal me. I hardly spoke, but I participated in all the activities, and each one planted seeds of grace. My heart was beginning to open up just a crack, but that tiny crack was all that God needed.

By early Saturday afternoon, we began to think about our children, not as dismembered nightmare babies, but as real children, with a face, name and a unique personality. We lit candles, naming the child and placing the candles in a bowl of water symbolizing the Well of Jacob and new life in Christ. For the first time instead of emptiness and rage I felt grief, and the tears slowly began to flow.

I had the sense that the aborted baby was a girl, and I named her Elizabeth. The next exercise which takes place early Saturday evening is an especially beautiful meditation where you are walking out of a dark forest and into a beautiful meadow where children are playing with Jesus. Before this retreat I would have had trouble believing such a thing, but during this meditation I had a very real encounter with a little girl playing in that meadow. As she approached me, I knew in my heart that this was my Elizabeth. In the meditation she seemed to be around 3 or 4 years old, but in another way her face was timeless and ageless, like an angel. She looked intently in my eyes, and I could feel that she was communicating something to me, not with words, but in my heart.

I could feel my heart open up with love for her during the course of the evening as I prayed and wrote a letter to her to be read at the memorial service the next day. I came to better understand what she spoke to my heart during that meditation:

> *"I still need you to be my Daddy. But as long as your heart is imprisoned by hatred and revenge, there is no way for me to enter your heart, so you can embrace me as your daughter. We cannot love each other the way I want to be loved. I still want you to be my father and to claim me as your own, and love me as your child."*

From the innocent heart of a child, denied life by my weakness, came the truth of my healing. If I remained consumed with hatred and thoughts of revenge, I would stay locked in that prison of pain and possibly hurt someone or more likely, myself. No one could get close to me, and I wouldn't let any one in. Now my wall of rage and hatred were being dismantled, and my heart was softening and the tears could flow. I could face the searing pain that lay beneath my rage, the deep grief at participating in the death of my little girl, and how much I missed her. But I was also filled with great consolation, because I knew that she was alive in the Lord, that we could have a spiritual relationship, and that we would be re-united in some way in eternity, God willing. This was such a healing realization for me! This was such a gift, a gift that without exaggeration saved my life!

Since that retreat, I participated in a men's Bible study at my church. I have come to realize that my anger at Janet was really not fair. God has given men a great responsibility, and we need to protect and provide for the women and children the Lord entrusts to us. That protection begins by offering them the commitment and stability of marriage before entering into a sexual relationship. I put her in that crisis by having sex with her without offering her the security of a commitment. She was vulnerable as a single mom, wanting the love and companionship of a man, but also in the position that another baby out of wedlock led her to see abortion as the only solution. Yes, it's true that Janet has her own responsibility in all this and I pray for the healing of her post abortion grief. But having sex outside of God's plan, placed Janet and eventually the child we conceived, at risk.

I wrote a letter to Janet and apologized for my role in the abortion. I shared with her about my retreat, and gave her resources for healing.

I continue to learn more about my Christian faith and God's will for my life.

I have days where I miss my daughter, yet I live with the hope that when my life is ended I will once again see the precious face of that little girl I met on that special Saturday evening of my Rachel's Vineyard Retreat, when she reached out to this wounded sinner and called me, "Daddy."

Chapter Seven
How Did I Get So Far From Who I Am?

By Daniel Smith

You know, some of the most significant events of our lives pass without us even recognizing them. That's how it was with me nearly 25 years ago when Ann, my girlfriend, aborted our child. It may sound as though she bears the full responsibility for this decision, but that is not the truth. I have come to understand that I too share responsibility for what happened that autumn many years ago.

As I think back, the decision to abort was made one dark night in November. Lying in bed together, she asked me a question. She said, "Hypothetically, if I told you that I was pregnant, what would you want to do?" Fear gripped me at that moment for, as I thought, this can't be happening to me---this is the end of my freedom, of my fun. This is the beginning of responsibility. I'm too young. I want to live before having children and getting married. After all, I was having fun with my friends and I did not want it to end.

It was then that the Devil entered into me. You see, the verse from the Bible where it says that the Devil entered into Judas is so true.

> "'I tell you the truth, one of you is going to betray me.' His disciples stared at one another, at a loss to know which of them he meant. One of them, the disciple whom Jesus loved, was reclining next to him."

Simon Peter motioned to this disciple and said, `Ask him which one he means.' Leaning back against Jesus, he asked him, `Lord, who is it?'

Jesus answered, `It is the one to whom I will give this piece of bread when I have dipped it in the dish.' Then dipping the piece of bread, he gave it to Judas Iscariot, son of Simon.

As soon as Judas took the bread, Satan entered into him."
John 13:21-27.

I lived that last verse. For the words that came from me, while said with my voice, were not mine. They were cold and murderous and calculating. Satan entered into me, but only because I let him.

I replied to Ann, "I would want you to have an abortion." I sealed my son's fate by the way I held her. My arms cradled her with one hand even touching her belly where rested our son of barely six weeks.

Later that night, I did wake up, and I do remember asking Ann if she was pregnant. She murmured, "No, Daniel, I'm not pregnant." Then she said to go back to sleep. There was no further discussion that night or the next day. The next time we would even broach the subject of being parents, it was too late.

Right before Thanksgiving Day, she said she had to drive somewhere and would not be at work. That was the day our son died. We did not realize it at the time, but that was also the day our relationship died. A relationship that held so much promise, and so much hope, and that was so much to both of us.

When we had first started dating, one day we sat and played one of those electronic games that today seem so simple. It may have been any of a number of the video games just coming out, but I remember sitting with Ann at the game board as I was turning the knobs, pressing the buttons, and becoming excited with anticipation of a high score. In the midst of it all, I looked up and into her eyes. And in those eyes, I saw a mirth, a goodness, a simplicity, a completion. In those eyes I saw our children. For her part, Ann told me that she loved me. She said that I was the brightest star, and that the sun rose and set on me.

We finished each other's sentences. We spent day and night talking. We smiled and laughed at everything. We saw movies, we ate our meals together, we traveled. We helped each other. Nothing was too much. Nothing was too little. The world was young, the days were golden, all was good, and we were together. And we had sex. Not thinking of marriage, or of commitment, or of the consequences of what we did, other than to make sure we were using some sort of contraception. Thinking back now, the sex started to take over for me. It seemed to become the most important part of the relationship. And sex was always very important for Ann.

How is it that we were able to lose sight of the most important reason we were attracted to each other? How is it that sex came to blind us to what really mattered?

Early on, we sat and discussed a book Ann read where the two characters, Sap and Lola, were all about having sex. This was exciting stuff, especially for a young guy who had been raised in a Catholic home, attended Catholic grade school, high school and even the University of Notre Dame. Yet at the same time, even though we did not know it, we were under attack. All around us were messages that said sex is good, sex is fun, sex is natural. Magazines, music, and books told us that if it feels good, do it. We saw the leading man and the leading woman in the movies having sex with each other even though they weren't married to each other. It was in every movie, now that I think back, except perhaps for some of the war movies. So, we thought, it must have been okay. And as a young guy in America in the 1970s and 1980s, you were expected to have sex—your virility was measured by the number of women you had. Women wanted sex anyway was the conventional wisdom. You just had to find the right words and make the right moves and you could be with any "chick" you wanted.

Of course, no one told us, no one showed us, where all of this "free love," this sexual liberation, would lead us. No one showed the hurt feelings, the broken hearts, the shattered dreams, the suffering, and the years of pain and emptiness. No one showed us the truth.

The Years of Darkness

Have you ever asked your loved one, or have you heard someone else ask, "What would I do without you?" Or, have you ever said, "I cannot imagine my life without you"?

Well, I, and I dare say, others, who have lost children and the mothers of our children to abortion, know the answers to these questions. These are not such idle musings. And that answer is an emptiness broken by strife, and infused with sorrow.

About two weeks after the abortion, Ann and I were talking on the phone. I cannot remember what prompted the call, but I do remember Ann saying that things had been taken care of. I asked her what she meant, and soon it became clear that she had had an abortion. With that realization, there echoed in my soul the condemnation of the Evil One. For I felt him say, "Now you are no longer innocent. You have done the unforgivable."

We still dated -- got together, stayed over, had sex (we had to wait a while after the abortion), talked, watched movies. But things were different. Perhaps, as the saying goes, the bloom was off the rose. We did not quite understand it all. But the reality was that our child, the union of the two of us, the best part of the both of us, was destroyed. And we had done it. Together.

This loss was just under the surface though at times it would surface. One of these first times was in January. On our way to an exhibition, while I was driving, she started to cry. I pulled over. She said through tears, "I wanted that child." I held her close to me. She cried on my right arm, staining the shirt with her mascara laced tears. (I kept that shirt with those stains for many years thereafter, but somehow it was lost along the way.) I did not know what to say. All I could say was that it will be okay. I was being brave, but I didn't know what to do or what would happen. After all, I did not know how deeply I, too, had been cut by it all.

In the months that followed, we could not discuss the abortion, the loss of our son, in any real way. There was either a fleeting reference to it, or a dismissal with a turn of phrase, or yelling and shouting and accusations. Our relationship started to wither. More time apart, less understanding, more fights and ugly silences. We started dating other people.

We no longer took pleasure in each other's company. We no longer could talk about everything, and, oddly enough, we, who had spoken so much of so many things, could not speak of this most important event in our lives.

Indeed, we could hardly understand each other any more. I had an opportunity to move to another city, and took it. Before leaving, I gave Ann my class ring, a big move and one I have not taken with any other woman. It was a way to show we are bound together. Even though I was moving several hundred miles away, I told her that I could not imagine my life without her and asked her to move with me. She refused, and we drifted further apart. Somehow, we both sensed that the best had come and gone.

Finally, even this bizarre dance, this strained relationship, came to an end. Within a matter of months, she had met and married another. It was something that became ever more likely as we fought more on the phone, never visited each other, and the ring was returned. The personal devastation that followed was not unexpected, either. Looking back, this was bound to be the result. A wave of despair engulfed me. The despair included physical pain and a withdrawal from everyone around me. I took time off from my job and spent days away from friends and family. I often went for long walks or camping trips in the woods and surrounding countryside. The pain was in every fiber of my being, during the hours I was awake, and even during my sleep. There was no respite. There was no end in sight. I had lost the love of my life. I knew it, and felt it and did not know how I would live with it. I despaired.

When you do not have a relationship with Him, then you turn to the things of the flesh. And in America of the late 20th century (and of today), that means devolving into sexual license. So following the dominant culture, I turned to sex with several women and to partying as a way to deaden my feelings. But it didn't. I m thankful for not falling into drug abuse or alcoholism as a way to deaden the pain.

In every face… I looked for Ann…hoping against hope. I took on the burden of carrying the full responsibility for the abortion, believing it to be all my fault, telling no one, and carrying the weight of it all.

Into the Light

We have all been in situations where we dread looking at the damage. It may be when we back our new car into a pole and feel the thud. Or it could be when a project at work "goes south" and we have to tell the boss. Or when we find our girlfriend is going out with our best friend. Or it could be when we lose our son or daughter to an abortion.

Things become more complicated when it comes to abortion. You see, we have always been told by the powerful in this society that abortion is a right, a woman's right. And we were never told by these people that abortion hurts people -- after all, they wouldn't allow it if it did hurt people or if it was bad for us. Would they? And, since abortion is a woman's issue and it is good, men should feel okay about it. Well, at least men should not feel bad when an abortion happens. Or, so goes the logic.

But men do naturally feel bad about losing children to abortion, and so they think there is something wrong with them for feeling this way, and so they stay quiet. Drawing ever more into themselves or reaching ever more frequently for distractions, they try to make it day to day.

The thing is, this approach of denying what happened and our feelings from it, takes a lot of energy because it means hiding from things-especially hiding from yourself. Denial, someone said, is a form of self-protection. And it works, rather nicely, too. It insulates us from emotions that we are not prepared to handle. It buys us time...for a while. Denial cannot last forever. It costs too much energy, it keeps us from healing, and so we are kept from living normally again.

Quite honestly, for years I simply avoided the subjects of losing Ann and the abortion. I kept it all locked away, but I knew where it was and I dreaded being near it. Any reminder or discussion of abortion or of Ann was quickly dispatched with frenetic activity. Even after confessing the sin of abortion to my parish priest, it all remained in the closet. With time, it pushed against the door, wanting to come out. Seeing no way for that to happen, anger started to build.

Dealing with the anger required that I accept what happened and put it all in its proper place. To do that, I had to face the events of the past, and, that in turn meant remembering everything. That is a difficult thing to do, and you must understand that the things I have written here were hidden from my conscious mind for nearly 20 years. That's a long time to carry a heavy load, but at some point it all becomes too wearisome, and you want to put it down.

For me, that point was reached during a crisis. It was too much to deal with--the struggle on the inside at the same time as the struggle on the outside.

The first step to laying down this rock was confronting it all, and that was hard. I could not have done it without the help of a good, trusted friend. Someone who kindly listened. So, in this kind of environment, for the first time, I looked at perhaps the most significant events of my life. I remembered the days, the evenings, the words, the events of all those years ago. I remembered things I thought I had forgotten. And with this, I saw how Ann and I really were, and the myths disappeared. Gone was the belief that I was all at fault. Oh, I had my faults. But Ann had hers, too. Together we had serious communications problems, to name just one of our matual problem. And we lived in a time and a place that affected both of us.

I remembered what she told me about her past. I remember how she grew up. And I began to read how this can affect someone. So I started to see her as a human being. Not as a goddess anymore. I started to put together the pieces of the puzzle of more than 20 years ago, in a place far away.

And, I took a hard look at myself and discovered some interesting things. I grew up in a Roman Catholic family with an emphasis on life. I went to Catholic grade school, high school, and college. Yet I was a hedonist. She came from a community that highly valued children. She wanted children, and I needed children. How could we allow the abortion to happen? How did we get here, to this place of desolation, so far from who we were? The answer is that we lived in a time and a place.

Unbeknownst to both of us, competing with these ideas, interfering with our ability to clearly see and understand, was an alien viewpoint that would profoundly influence us and sear our lives. One way to describe these forces would be to call them a materialism that reduced all things to the here and the now and which placed us, as individuals, with our pleasures and desires, at the center of everything. This could also be called a radical individual autonomy that separated each of us from all around except for what they may be able to offer us. And with this individualism came a separation from those before us, those to come after us, and those in our own family. We were isolated from the sources of our lives and so could fall for anything. These realizations showed the depth of my hurt, and, I dare say, showed the hurt of others. These flashes of understanding revealed the icy cold emptiness that had been my life, and the pathways of death I had walked for so long.

These nefarious ideas did not simply fall out of the sky. They came to us through the movies, the classrooms, the books and magazines that we encountered on a daily basis. They came to us because someone, somewhere, made the decision that these ideas, these values, were the ones we would receive. It was years later after having read the work of Catholic scholars like Gerry Bradley and Michael Jones that I came to see that the myths which we grew up, that we surrounded ourselves with late in 20th Century USA, were just that –myths. Or, to be more blunt, lies.

As young men and women, we came to believe and accept that somehow we were building a new world, a free world. And, that we were freer and smarter than at any other time in history. We were told there was a "we," all Americans are one big family, and we believed it. But reality was different, as it always is in times of delusion.

Smarter? No, we were just arrogant and ignorant of the sophisticated means by which we were being manipulated. Freer? No, just promiscuous and isolated. And where were those responsible for teaching us, and preparing us for life? Where were the shepherds who were to protect the flock?

Once we left the arms of our parents, we were entrusted to stewards who were to teach us and warn us. But they did not. Looking back, it is clear that a Catholic high school religion class was reduced to black and white photographs of potholes half filled with water or groups of inner city kids standing around and talking. At the place some call the preeminent Catholic university we were immersed in the sex and booze and the rock and roll of the destructive mainstream American society. In loco parentis, in place of our parents, was what the administration at the University of Notre Dame told us was their role...but that wasn't so. They were wolves in sheep's clothing. Abortion? Never heard of it. Sex outside of marriage? It was tacitly approved. At a time when abortion was quadrupling, those with a voice and a duty to use that voice were derelict in protecting their young charges. They either did not believe, or they sold out.

Awakening to the reality that was Ann and Daniel more than 20 years ago, and awakening to the truth of our surroundings so long ago, caused pain. But from pain can come wisdom, understanding, and freedom. And that brings healing and wholeness…and peace.

Healing and Health

When we break our bones or cut ourselves, we can't do what we used to do. We have to heal before we can go back to our normal activities. The body must first regenerate itself, and that happens with the proper care and attention over time. When we suffer an emotional, or a spiritual loss, we are wounded, and that wound has to heal. When you are young, you are made of steel and rubber, and you think that you can endure anything, that you can live through everything, that there are no mistakes, that you will liver forever. But that is not so as time teaches us.

The American Heritage Dictionary defines "health" as the "optimal functioning with freedom from disease and abnormality", and "healing" is defined as restoring to the condition of normality. For us humans, that means that we put things in their place after having properly dealt with them. After the abortion, for me that meant grieving the loss of my little son as well as the loss of my dearest Ann. It meant accepting these losses, and accepting the loss of the family with Ann that He meant us to have at one time. It meant accepting all of these things and the emptiness in me, and offering it up for His purposes.

This healing process, this process of grieving and acceptance did not occur in one weekend, or in a week, or in a month. Even after facing the events of long ago, I had to deal with the rage that comes from the knowledge of the reality of what happened. This anger does not easily drain because at the base of it is the sense that we have been emasculated for not protecting our own flesh and blood. With time, that empty chair, that silent room, the hole in my soul left by the loss of this child and his mother, took root in me, and I came to realize that this loss was permanent.

Going to Confession, reading tirelessly about abortion, working feverishly in the pro-life movement, being nice to people. These things did not bring me back to health. If anything, they caused me to ask, "Why doesn't anyone seem to care about my little one and his mommy?" (For I sensed that Ann, too, must have grievously suffered this loss.)

I learned that I had a Father in heaven who did care and learned that healing would take years of prayer and hard work. By opening myself to this conversation with the Lord, His life and warmth filled me and lead me back to the Roman Catholic Faith, from which I had traveled so far. The Faith provides the way to live, not just **a** way to live. I came to understand that sex, in any form, outside of marriage is simply a very bad thing.

The Faith, I came to realize, explains the reason for living. For so long I believed money, power, pleasure, and sex were all that there was. But these things really mean nothing, and achieving these things is not the goal, or reason, of life.

It is amazing to me now as I look back, of the skewed values I held. I feared a home and a hearth with a family thinking it was bondage, not knowing how enslaving the loneliness without this family would be. I was more concerned with not hurting the feelings of a Black man than I was in saving the life of my child. I was more aware of the Holocaust of the Jews in World War II than of the holocaust that took the life of my son and the lives of tens of millions children. I looked in the mirror everyday as I shaved, yet did not know this same visage would somehow be reflected in my son's face. There I stood, defending a country of barely 200 years yet I could not understand that my child was the member of a family and of a people stretching back for centuries, and an heir to a tradition that was given to us by God Himself. I risked my health and life to defend the same country that allowed my son to be cruelly put to death and destroyed what should have been my family. An American abortionist killed my little boy and ruined the relationship between Ann and I. It is sobering to realize how Ann and I were the targets of what I can only now call a war – a war against people, a war against families, a war against Truth. And this war was carried on by deception in turning Ann and I against each other, and the two of us against our son.

This reflection on what was, this understanding of the awful truth of the lives of Ann and I and of our troubling surroundings, this is all so freeing. For I no longer hold just myself accountable for this unspeakable tragedy. Where once there was anger towards Ann, it is replaced by a gentle hope for her well-being. Where there was a desire to get back what is lost, there is a relinquishment and a release of all that happened and an entrustment to Him to let Him do with it as He will. I understand now that Ann and I lived in a time and a place, and that time and place shaped what we did. Those who created the toxic culture that gave our son less than an even chance must bear responsibility for the little one's death, and for our suffering.

This has allowed me to move forward, and to live maturely, responsibly, and with strength. To seek Him in all that I do. To listen to those around me for the cry of help, the whisper of need, the laughter of joy. It has allowed me to understand the reality of the situation in which we find ourselves in this society, this culture of death. The reality is that men and women shape and govern this society divorced from the fundamental values concerning sexuality and the dignity of the unborn child, shared by Catholics and other Christians alike. They remain blind to the great suffering of women, and men, who weep for their children and what may have been.

Through my suffering and loss, I have come to see clearly how abortion, and the culture of death that surrounds it, must, and will one day be brought to an end. That answer is the conversion of hearts and minds to the truth that abortion not only ends the life of a unique unborn child, but also deeply wounds all who participate in it. With the conversion of hearts and minds to the truth that God has placed in each of our hearts, souls may be saved as lives are lead in accordance with the only true purpose of this life– to know, love and serve God so as to be with Him in the next life.

The answer is not blowing in the wind. The answer is His Truth, the Faith. The answer is being His children.

Chapter Eight
Amazing Grace:
Sexual Addiction and Abortion

By Ian Stewart

I was born in Lincoln, Nebraska.

I was raised in a lower middle class family and have a brother, six years older, and a sister, two years older. My father was a precision machinist, but lost his job and had to take a job as a janitor for the State Department of Roads for the last years of his life. He was a very ill man with a heart condition and diabetes among other things. He was a gentle man, a good father, and from my perception, a good husband. He died at age 58, gently, in his sleep.

My mother, I have since found out, was sexually abused as a child and young adult. She had an eighth grade education, so worked part and full-time menial jobs to help pay the bills. She lived to 80 plus years and passed away after a struggle with liver cancer.

We had little, but my Dad's brother grew vegetables and fruits on his acreage. We visited him frequently during the summer months and loaded the car with the "fruits of the field". At home, we all pitched in and helped to can and freeze them for the winter. All three of us kids had to help do the processing, which was long and arduous work. But, we knew that would help get us through the winter.

We were raised Lutheran and attended church and Sunday school regularly. I had 11 years of perfect attendance, including the time I assisted in teaching Sunday school.

I had a good work ethic as taught to me by my father—watching him. He was a hard worker. I could earn extra money mowing lawns (my father helped me purchase a used gas-powered mower, and I paid him back with the profits). In the wintertime, I removed snow from walks with a shovel.

When I was 11 ½ years old, my older brother molested me. This was one of the most memorable and life-changing experiences of my life. I was too young to be able to handle this powerful emotion and as you will see as my story unfolds, this led to the development over the years of a sexual addiction. The molestation continued for about six months--until my brother went into the service.

I grew to crave this sexual release—much like a heroine addict and began to masturbate regularly. It was such a comfort for all the loneliness, let downs, put-downs, silence, and being "ignored". The kids teasing me at school in the sixth grade didn't bother me, because now, I could "feel good" when I got home. For that short period of time, I could be in control and feel good; I could shut out all of those negative feelings. The masturbation got to be a habit, which grew into an addiction—but I did not realize it had escalated to that degree. It took away my loneliness, even if for only a short while. It made me feel mentally and emotionally strong and powerful. I thought to myself, "What could be better than what I am feeling?" I was hooked! I really didn't know how to handle this "powerful medicine."

Since I entertained myself much of the time through grade school, I became a loner. I was a loner and was used to doing things by myself, so this self-sex fit in to my life very comfortably. I had only one male friend at a time through high school. I became self-centered and self-reliant. I nurtured the relationship of self instead of others. I was interested in sex, but I wouldn't push the girl to have sex. I would accept when she stopped my advances and take care of myself when I was alone.

After high school, I attended college at University of Nebraska-Lincoln. Unfortunately, I had to drop out of the University due to my father's illness (heart attack). I then obtained employment at an electronics manufacturing plant in Lincoln. I started on the assembly line and moved up to Parts Expediter, then to Head Parts Expediter in the year I was employed there, prior to getting my draft notice from Uncle Sam (this was during the Vietnam war).

I met my future wife Nicole when she had just turned 15 and I was 19 ½. It was a short time later that I received my draft notice. I thought my time in the service would be a good opportunity to advance my education. I was extremely interested in electronics as a vocation. I explained to Nicole she should date others while I was in the service, but we would write letters and I would see her when I came home on leave.

Relationships for me continued to be difficult and few. Sexuality was mainly self-sex. Since I was fearful of getting a girl pregnant I avoided sex. In fact, I pretty much avoided being with the opposite sex at all. Part of me wanted to be promiscuous, but I was afraid of sexually transmitted diseases and getting a girl pregnant.

I never lost sight of Nicole and we stayed in touch. She was gorgeous and I was enamored by her youthfulness and beauty and I longed for her much of the time. Nicole's interest in me made me feel important and respected, which made me feel very good about myself. She admired me. We were the same religion, we could talk to each other comfortably, and those were big plusses for her.

During one of my visits home from the Navy, Nicole and I had sex. We were both virgins. It was somewhat awkward for both of us.

Nicole was still young and after graduating from high school, pursued training away from home, and moved to the East Coast to work. Meanwhile, I was on the West Coast and deployed on a ship overseas. We wrote letters fairly regularly which decreased over time, though we still communicated on major holidays and birthdays.

Nicole experienced her first abortion during this time. It was after a date rape when she was 20. I wouldn't learn of this until 30 years later.

While I was stationed on shore duty in the South, Nicole came to visit for several days. I asked her if she wanted to get married-

-she declined. I think she was involved in a promiscuous lifestyle that I later learned was part of the acting out that can follow a traumatic rape and abortion.

I was transferred to the East Coast and Nicole took a job overseas in the Far East. We were still many miles apart. She continued in her wild times, while I continued to "take care of myself" sexually and became emotionally distant from any relationships.

I had been in the service for a little over ten years when we were finally reunited, decided this was "fate", and we should get married. During the planning for our wedding she felt something just wasn't right with our relationship—it looked good on the outside, but didn't feel right on the inside. Nevertheless, we married and spent the next ten years in the Navy moving from place to place.

Two years into the marriage she became aware of my mistress… pornography. At that time she was unable to approach me about it and suffered in silence.

When I retired from the military, we moved back to the Midwest. Times were rocky for most of our marriage. It would be another 13 years before I would be diagnosed as having a sex addiction. We went to several counselors but they all told Nicole she was just making a mountain out of a molehill and "that pornography is what guys do. It's not like he was having an 'affair' or anything like that."

This addiction to pornography took its toll on our relationship. I had books, magazines, and videos all locked up and stashed in a footlocker – you know, so the kids wouldn't get to them. I knew they shouldn't be looking at that stuff and reading those stories. I really didn't think it was wrong for me to look at those pictures and videos and read those books; and even the masturbation wasn't a big deal to me. All the counselors seemed to agree when they said, "What's the big deal?"

We were becoming more distant in our relationship. My lying increased. Yeah, I lied to Nicole as well as myself. I became more indifferent to Nicole and her constant "nagging". All I needed was to find some excuse to be alone and get into my medication for my addiction, and then I would "feel better". I also started working longer hours – just to stay away from the strife at home. As it turned out that was not the right answer to the situation either.

My older brother was married and lived in a city about 45 minutes away. He would come to visit on occasions. I really didn't think too much of it when he would be at our house when I arrived home from work. Now, knowing much more about sex addiction, I realize that this should have been a blazing red flag. My brother also was a sex addict… and he was pursuing my wife.

Nicole, a stay at home mom at this time, was in an extremely vulnerable position. She was busy with our three children in grade school but lonely and isolated because of our distant relationship. She was friendly toward my brother, he knew her schedule, so he preyed upon her until opportunity presented itself. Nicole and my brother conceived a child. They made the plans for an abortion and she went ahead with it without my knowledge.

Several years later, Nicole's guilt overcame her and she told me about the affair and the abortion and asked me for forgiveness. She did not share that my brother was the father of the baby until later in our healing journey. I believe it was God's grace that allowed me to forgive her, but I was also very numb to emotions and relationships because of my addiction. She was hopeful that our marriage relationship would get better, but it did not.

Chaos and isolation continued to prevail.

Our sex life had become virtually non-existent. Nicole had little or no desire regarding sex; at least sex with me. I became emotionally anorexic (totally indifferent) toward relationships.

We both had our own secrets. These secrets were shame and guilt based. We were not honest with one another and our communication was superficial and weak. We went along day-by-day with small talk. We were getting mired down in the muck, like having a millstone around our neck being dragged down into the waters of despair. Our relationship was stagnant, we felt we were drowning, but couldn't put a finger on "how".

This was a very dark time in our relationship. I had a problem with honesty that led me to lose my job, which I dearly loved. That set us back financially and also added more stress to an already fragile relationship.

I found a lower paying job as an electronics assembler in a factory on the assembly line. During this time, God reached down with his hand of love and compassion and lifted us up. To this day we don't know how the Lord orchestrated that . . . but He did as He opened our eyes to His grace.

We began to tithe (a tithe is personal income set apart as an offering to God or for works of mercy). We found ourselves with bills getting paid and getting out of debt, even though I had a much lower paying job than before. Our relationship didn't get worse, but it didn't get much better, either.

Nicole started listening to Christian radio and found information about sexual addiction. She finally was able to put a label about her disconcerted feelings regarding our relationship . . . I was addicted to pornography. I acted out by masturbating. She pursued this newfound information with counseling appointments, phone calls, etc. Nicole spent another two years gathering information. It seems the counselors she talked to knew little about "sex addiction."

She finally found a counselor that understood this condition and offered treatment. He told Nicole that he would see me only if I would set up the appointment. I was very hesitant. I didn't call for a couple of days. Then I thought, "What's the problem, he'll probably say the same as all the other counselors". I called. He answered (as I found out later, this was highly unusual as the receptionist takes all incoming calls). He had a quiet and comforting voice. I made an appointment.

Nicole and I attended the first session together. From that "interview" I was diagnosed beyond any doubt with a pornography problem and I had a choice: start recovery or lose virtually everything. I decided to start recovery. I visited the counselor regularly and I seemed to make progress. He noticed I responded favorably to a spiritual bent on recovery so he asked if I would like to approach this addiction from a spiritual aspect. I affirmed that would be very beneficial to me.

In the beginning stages of my recovery, Nicole asked me if I had ever been molested. I shared with Nicole about my brother's molestation and the origins of my sexual addiction.

Nicole finally felt the courage to share the truth about her second abortion: my brother was the father of that child. She knew it couldn't be my baby since I had had a vasectomy after the birth of our third child. I told her I would have been able to accept this baby as our own. I was very sad to hear what my brother had done and sad my wife was unable to come to me. She said she felt trapped and afraid to face me at the time.

To be fair to Nicole, the truth is that my addiction to pornography virtually drove her into this adulterous situation. Had I been more loving and emotionally involved in her life, I am sure this would not have happened. I have since realized that the "paper dolls" were a form of adultery or idol worship. It was my mistress for all of our marriage until I entered recovery.

Nicole realized that she needed healing of her abortion trauma and loss. Through a friend she found out about a program offered through Catholic Social Services called Project Rachel. She found that program to be very helpful. It was during this time that she shared with me, for the first time, about the rape and her first abortion. I felt grief and sorrow for Nicole and the baby she aborted. She named that child but asked me if I'd name the second child aborted. I remember that was an evening filled with tears and holding each other and crying.

Then she found that the Crisis Pregnancy Center in town held a Bible Study for men and women that were post-abortive. When she asked if I would attend with her, I didn't hesitate and said, "Yes". We attended that Bible Study together for about ten weeks. It was very good. The book I used was *Healing a Father's Heart.* [7] It was very informational, and very compassionately done.

By this time I was in early recovery for my pornography addiction and struggling as most do in early recovery. I was attending a 12-Step group for sex addiction. It was very encouraging and helpful. I was beginning to understand some of the dynamics that cause this addictive behavior. Our relationship was starting to slowly improve. I read many books on sex addiction and how pornography eats away at the soul as a cancer eats away in the body.

---

[7] Linda Cochrane and Kathy Jones, *Healing a Fathers Heart: A Post-Abortion Bible Study for Men* (Baker Books, 1996)

I was beginning to understand how my addiction had been a catalyst to drive my wife into another's arms. It had taken me away physically, mentally and spiritually. I was humbled. We started doing things we rarely or never had done before—together. Like dating, praying out loud and reading the Bible together, having more friends and getting together to do things, planning things as a couple, planning activities as a group, making purchases for the house (together!) and having more quality time with our kids.

A year after Nicole went through Project Rachel with a counselor, this counselor told Nicole about Rachel's Vineyard Weekend Retreats for healing after abortion. She felt that Nicole would really benefit by going.

Nicole decided to attend the retreat. I was amazed at the difference in her when she arrived home after that weekend. She could not say enough great things about the weekend, about the women she had met, and the deep forgiveness she experienced from God. It was like the first spring day after a harsh winter hearing her speak about the weekend. She didn't go into great detail, but shared how she felt the Holy Spirit amongst the group and the forgiveness that abounded.

Nicole decided to get involved in helping to facilitate other Rachel's Vineyard weekends. She is a very good administrator. The leaders of the group needed that kind of assistance to coordinate, plan, schedule and do the administrative work necessary to have a smoother, more successful retreat weekend.

She helped with a weekend several months later. Nicole then asked, "Ian, would you be willing to go on a RV weekend with me in another city?" I agreed. If I had not been in recovery, I would have declined. Since I had been in recovery I knew I should attend – for us. I was actually quietly excited to attend, but still had some reservations. (Fear of the unknown.)

During the weekend I was amazed how I was able to fit in (there were a couple of other post-abortive men there). I saw the forgiveness transformation of several women before my very eyes. I will never be the same. I felt the Holy Spirit moving around, among and in us. God's presence was there with its entire splendor manifested in the power of healing forgiveness. It was beautiful.

The weekend was full of love, compassion and healing for all of us.

As the weekend progressed I could see how the Rachel's Vineyard Retreat was helping me to better understand the emotional experience of the women participants. I was also able to relate to this to my own experiencing of mercy and forgiveness from God for my sex addiction. I could feel the presence of God, once again moving my spirit. I was emotionally high; I was emotionally drained; but I was feeling my emotions! I was feeling the emotions of others; I was feeling more in touch and alive to the Holy Spirit. I realized my heart was communicating at a deeper level with God—that I was getting—in touch…with myself and with my God. All of this from an emotionally anorexic person—it was a miracle to me. Nicole noticed it too, though she was still dealing with her emotions on a deeper level too.

The most revealing part of the weekend to me was coming in contact in the beautiful "living scripture meditations" featured in the retreat process, with our two unborn babies that are waiting for us in heaven. It reminds me of the story of *Tilly* by Frank E. Peretti and the drama produced by Focus on the Family, of the same name.

I have since realized that through the mercy and power of God all of this has worked out for our total benefit! We have found forgiveness and healing in the loving arms of God. We both have found a deeper and healthier relationship with each other. We have placed our secrets in the open and have talked about them. Looking back, once those secrets were "on the table" we were able to start communicating at a deeper level and the shame, anger, guilt, and pain began to subside.

At our Rachel's Vineyard Retreat, I was moved to write a poem as a tribute to our unborn son and daughter that I read at the memorial service held on Sunday of our retreat:

Christian Paul

Christian Paul was our adopted son
Adopted through Christ and no other one.
A baby so sweet that we really miss;
A baby so sweet that we'll never kiss.
Ah, but we'll see him in another place,
We'll see him then face to face.
We'll thank him for his sacrifice
So we could grow and be real nice.
We are sorrowful; remorseful that you died,
T'was all our fault and many tears were cried
When we finally realized to ourselves we lied;
But you've gone ahead to be our guide!
What is it like Christian, what do you see?
Can you describe heaven to mom and me?
Are there clouds or rain or maybe sun?
Ah, you're so lucky for the prize you've won.
If there were love and peace on earth,
Living here would have more worth.
We are here learning to love and kiss,
But you are the one we really miss.
We're waiting for the happy day
When we'll join you along the way
To our move heavenward bound
Away from this painful earthly ground.
Christian, can you ever forgive
Our wicked choice to not let you live?
Tell us quick that, "It's really OK",
Then run along to Jesus and play.
Love,
Mom & Dad

Sarah Dawn

Sarah Dawn our love's delight,
It was great to see you Saturday night!
To see a vision of your face;
To see you alive through Jesus' Grace!
You know we are repentant for our sin.
Jesus forgives us so we'll see you again.
He showed us by vision of your fun
How you rollick and play in the Son.
God is gracious for giving us, you,
Then being your parent for us, too!
We long to be with you someday
God planned it to happen just that way.
Though we really messed up and did things wrong,
We know your forgiveness didn't take very long
'Cause Jesus taught you on the day you met
Your parents do love you and they do regret
The choice they made in eighty-seven
That sent their girl straight to Heaven
To wait for them, to mature—grow up
It was their time to drink from the bitter cup.
We're sorry it happened just this way,
Your sacrifice for us on that gray day!
But now we're healing from that grief
Forgiveness from God is our relief!
Love,
Mom and Dad

Chapter Nine
Lazarus Revisited:
The Resurrection of a Marriage

By David and Susan

Susan and I separated several times; each of us had affairs during our troubled marriage. Our marriage was still on shaky ground when we arrived at the retreat center. We had finally come to the realization that it wasn't so much a marriage problem between us as it was an abortion problem. We didn't know how to get past the barrier that abortion placed between us. We were empty, lonely and unable to reach out and console each other in our secret pain.

One of the main reasons we stayed together was because of our children, born after our abortion. The abortion happened soon after we were married. I was in the Army and was called to complete my last year of service stationed in Germany. We agreed that Susan would stay with her folks. We would save our money, and she would begin looking at houses for when I returned. That was the plan.

Susan called me shortly after I began my duty overseas and shared that she was pregnant. The first thing I told her was, "We're not ready for this; I have to finish my service. We can't do this with me away for the next year." I convinced her that abortion was the right decision.

The day of the abortion was the day I died. I felt dead for 14 years.

When I returned home I struggled to understand myself as husband and provider. I knew deep down that I had rejected my first child and I felt like such a hypocrite. I spent four years of my life defending this country, but couldn't prevent the death of my child because of fear, inconvenience, and selfishness. Like a lot of men, I dealt with this wound…by not dealing with it. I stuffed it down deep, and put all my energy into my work. I felt like my identity was taken from me and I never felt whole.

I was successful in my business, but I had this nagging sense that disaster was just over the horizon and couldn't enjoy or trust anything good in my life. I had a wife, a nice house, and a couple of beautiful children. But I never felt whole. It was like something was missing.

I worked all the time and was emotionally distant from my wife and kids. I felt in many ways like an outsider; more like a hired caretaker without a deep bond with my family. When this painful realization would break through I would drink, look at porn on the internet, and try to get away from these feelings as quickly as possible. But this denial was slowly eating away at my marriage and robbed me of the gifts that surrounded me-gifts that I was unable to fully embrace and celebrate.

Susan and I both turned to people outside our relationship to help ease the loneliness and pain we secretly carried in our hearts. The only way we knew how to share our grief, was through toxic angry exchanges that only left us more alienated, more hurt, more alone. So we looked for others to meet our physical and emotional needs and had affairs with friends and co-workers. Unfortunately it is not hard to find other lonely wounded people who are acting out their own unhealed pain. I think broken people have special emotional radar that helps them find each other.

Despite our struggles, we clung to our Christian faith, even as we fell short and sinned, and tried to make things work for the sake of the children. We started to see a Christian counselor at our church. For the first time, someone asked us if there was an abortion in our past. Susan just broke down. It was clear that this was the greatest wound in our marriage, and the source of our marital struggles. If we were to stay together and build a new foundation in this marriage, we had to face this loss, and all the dark feelings associated with it. The counselor recommended a weekend retreat for post abortion healing called Rachel's Vineyard. We found their website and registered for the next retreat in our area.

We arrived at the retreat center very anxious of what was to come, but quietly excited and hopeful that maybe this would help in some way. If it didn't, I was sure our marriage was headed for divorce.

The Rachel's Vineyard Retreat is a healing process that uses various activities and exercises that are specially designed to heal the deeply buried grief and other pain that arises from an abortion loss. One of the first activities of the retreat on Friday evening is based on the bible story of "The Woman Caught in Adultery." These scripture stories are "re enacted" in a process called "Living Scripture." In these meditations you enter the scripture story and become a participant in that event. Here's the story from John's Gospel:

> *Then the scribes and the Pharisees brought a woman who had been caught in adultery and made her stand in the middle. They said to him, "Teacher, this woman was caught in the very act of committing adultery. Now in the law, Moses commanded us to stone such women. So what do you say?" They said this to test him, so that they could have some charge to bring against him. Jesus bent down and began to write on the ground with his finger. But when they continued asking him, he straightened up and said to them, "Let the one among you who is without sin be the first to throw a stone at her." And in response, they went away one by one, beginning with the elders. So he was left alone with the woman before him. Then Jesus straightened up and said to her, "Woman, where are they? Has no one condemned you?" She replied, "No one, sir." Then Jesus said, "Neither do I condemn you. Go, (and) from now on do not sin any more." John 8, 3-11*

After the scripture meditation we pass a rock around the room. As we share the rock with the person seated next to us we ask them, "Does anyone here condemn you?"

They answer, "No."

I reply, "Neither do I condemn you, go and sin no more." This is repeated as the rock is passed establishing a sense of connection and safety in our group.

After the exercise, as we shared our experience of the meditation, we touched on the issue of self condemnation and were made aware of a pile of rocks of various sizes, shapes, colors and textures placed beneath a table at the center of the room. It turns out that many of us gathered on that retreat struggled with forgiving ourselves for our role in the death of our unborn children, and others struggled to forgive those who had pushed them to abort.

The retreat facilitator invited those of us struggling with forgiveness issues to carry a rock as a reminder — a symbol of condemnation — of our inability to forgive. The rock represented (in a very concrete way!) our conflict. At any point during the weekend, we could freely put it down. Until that time you were instructed to carry it with you at all times. Through this simple exercise I became aware as the retreat progressed, of how the burden of self-condemnation was impacting my life in so many ways and keeping me imprisoned in anger, depression and fear.

After I picked up my rock, I was inspired to share with the group, "I've been carrying this rock for 14 years. I've been emotionally dead for that long. I throw myself into my work, which alienates me from my wife, and it causes her to be angry, but I don't know what else to do. I don't know how to heal. We don't know how to heal our marriage."

Fortunately we were definitely in the right place. With each exercise and activity I began to trust that we were on a painful but rewarding journey that would bring the healing in our lives we so desperately longed for. By Saturday evening of the retreat we were experiencing abundant grace and the loving support of the retreat team and the other participants. For the first time we were able to share the story of our abortion experience, and felt safe to share our hearts with each other and the group.

On Saturday afternoon we participated in the Living Scripture exercise based on the story of Lazarus in the Gospel of John:

> *When Martha heard that Jesus was coming, she went out*
> *to meet him, but Mary stayed in the house. Martha said*
> *to Jesus, "If you had been here, Lord, my brother would*

not have died… When Mary arrived where Jesus was and saw him, she fell at his feet. "Lord," she said, "if you had been here, my brother would not have died!" Jesus saw her weeping, and the Jews who had come with her weeping also; his heart was touched, and he was deeply moved. "Where have you buried him?" he asked them. "Come and see, Lord," they answered.

Jesus wept…

Deeply moved… Jesus went to the tomb, which was a cave with a stone placed at the entrance. "Take the stone away!" Jesus ordered. …After he had said this he called out in a loud voice, "Lazarus, come out!" The dead man came out, his hands and feet wrapped in grave cloths, and a cloth around his face. "Untie him," Jesus told them, "and let him go." John 11

You are probably wondering how they reenacted this scripture account. The retreat participants are asked to name parts of themselves that have died because of sin. The facilitator then takes a strip of gauze bandage, and gently wraps the area we identify. Some in our group wrapped their eyes because they lost sight of God. One woman asked that her heart be wrapped as it was broken by abandonment of her father and later her boyfriend when she became pregnant. Another man felt powerless to stop an abortion he did not want and asked that his hands be wrapped.

When the retreat team approached Susan my wife decided to have her left hand wrapped. Susan said, "This is the hand that my wedding ring is on, and I want to see our marriage restored".

As the team approached me, I shared "You have to wrap my heart . . . it is just broken. It's been broken ever since I got the call that the abortion was over and my child was gone."

Each of us was then given the opportunity to profess our faith. Through faith in Christ we believe that we can rise from the death caused by sin and be healed of our deepest wounds. After Susan made her statement of faith a team member went to unwrap her bandage. I received a gift of grace at that moment that led me to say, "No, no, please, let me do it -- I think this is my place as her husband. I want a partnership to begin that we never have had. I want to be there for her, not so distant any more."

And so, I unwrapped her hand. Susan, in turn, unwrapped my heart and asked forgiveness for her bitterness toward me. We embraced for the longest time. It was as if all the distance, pain and loneliness between us melted away in that embrace; it was a timeless and blessed event. For the first time since we were dating, we held hands as we walked along the road together to the cafeteria for our evening meal.

I took back something very important when I unwrapped Susan's hand that day. I was reclaiming and embracing my God-given vocation as provider and protector of my wife. After the retreat, Susan expressed to me that she felt secure in our relationship, protected and loved.

Since that weekend retreat, we have been like a young couple growing in love with one another. We experience the growing pains that any couple faces, and the challenges that family life present us. But because of our healing, we are deeply connected to one another, and can openly share our hearts and souls. We have disagreements and we struggle at times. But we can have conflict without the pain and anguish that kept us from communicating effectively in the past... even about minor problems. We trust we will work through our problems together. I know we are better parents. Our children benefit so much for this new peace and stability in our marriage.

We are so grateful for the mercy and forgiveness of God. No matter how far we drift from God in our lives, not matter the ways we hurt others and ourselves through our sin and selfishness, our God is waiting for us to return to him. If you are suffering because abortion has touched your life, don't be afraid because our Creator is a loving Father who hungers for your return to His Heart.

The words of Jesus say it so beautifully:

> *But now we must celebrate and rejoice, because your brother was dead and has come to life again; he was lost and has been found.* (Luke 15,32)

Chapter Ten
Gina's Story

From *Forbidden Grief: The Unspoken Pain of Abortion*
By Theresa Burke

"I was hoping you could help my daughter. She needs counseling. Somebody objective. God certainly knows I'm not." Mr. Davis's voice trailed off as if in regretful thought.

"What's the problem?" I asked, shifting the telephone receiver to my shoulder so I could jot down a few notes.

"Well," he stammered, "my daughter, Gina, is dating this guy. He's verbally and physically abusive. He is ruining her life." Mr. Davis sounded desperate. In his voice I could detect anger and hurt but worst of all helplessness. "I can't just sit back and watch my daughter ruin her life. This guy already has another kid he can't support. I don't know what she sees in him. My Gina, she's a great girl."

His tone changed to a hushed whisper. "I love her so much but I'm losing her." He was silent for a moment, then his voice cracked, "Please, can you do something? Can you help her see what a creep he is? Gina won't listen to me anymore."

I informed Mr. Davis that I couldn't break them up but I could help Gina examine her relationship and sort out her feelings about this man. Then I asked Mr. Davis if anything else had happened between Gina and her boyfriend.

The question itself was a threat. Mr. Davis hesitated. Finally he answered, "Well, there is something but it should really come from her.

I think she should be the one to tell you. After all, it's her life and I don't want her to think I was talking behind her back."

"Did your daughter have an abortion?" I asked in a matter of fact tone. The word was said. Abortion. There was silence, as is almost always the case. I had a telephone listing for Rachel's Vineyard Retreats (for Post Abortion Healing), yet still people would often struggle to explain why they were calling.

I met his daughter that night. Gina was 19, with long blond hair and sad blue eyes. "My dad made me have it," she explained. "He told me I could not live with them if I didn't. He knew it might make me hate him but he was willing to take that risk. I'd get over it, he said. I was not raised to believe in abortion. In high school I even wrote a paper on it." Her eyes welled with tears, shining like brilliant sapphires.

For three years Gina had never told anyone about the abortion; within a few moments, the memory surfaced like a tidal wave of grief. The surges of the experience came crashing against the fortress of my therapeutic composure as I attempted to steady her for the next gush of emotion.

Gina's story came out in between distressing sobs and gasps for air. "I came home from college on a Friday to tell them about the pregnancy and what we were planning to do.... My dad hit the roof. He wanted to know what he ever did to deserve this. Dad took my boyfriend into the kitchen to have a man-to-man talk. They would not let me in. Dad tried to pressure him to convince me that abortion was the best thing."

With much difficulty, she continued. "Two days later I was up on a table, my feet in stirrups.... I cried the whole way there.... My mom took me.... I kept telling her I did not want this.... Please no! Don't make me do this; don't make me do this.... I said it the whole way there.... No one listened. When a counselor asked me if I was sure, I shrugged my shoulders.... I could hardly speak. They did it.... They killed my baby."

Overcome with heartache, Gina began to moan. Bent over holding her womb, she couldn't believe she had actually had an abortion. After a long tearful pause, Gina continued, "Just as quickly as it had happened everyone seemed to forget about it. My parents never talked about it. They were furious when they found out that I was still seeing Joe. They never let up on their negative comments about him. Things were not so good between Joe and me either. We were always fighting. I was so depressed and did not know how to handle my feelings. I was too ashamed to talk about the abortion with my friends, and my parents made me promise not to tell anyone."

As her story unraveled, I saw many signals of complicated mourning. Anger and hurt filled Gina's heart. There was grief too, tremendous grief over a dead baby who would never be there to offer joy and hope. Anything related to babies made her cry: baby showers, diaper commercials, even children. Everything triggered relentless heartache. There was a wound in her soul that simply would not stop bleeding.

Though Gina's family had been nominally Christian, religious faith did not hinder their desire for an abortion. Her parents had believed that by insisting on abortion they would save her from a life of poverty and tribulation with a man they did not believe could love or support their precious daughter. Joe already had a child whom he was not supporting. They feared for her future with such a man.

Now the future was here. Her self-esteem crumbled, depression was a constant companion, and her parents watched sadly as a negative transformation robbed them of the daughter they knew.

Gina needed permission to grieve. Her parents had deprived her of the genuine compassion and acceptance she needed from them. They had not accepted the pregnancy earlier; later they could not accept her grief. She felt utterly rejected by them.

Gina joined our support group and also came for individual therapy. Once in treatment for post-abortion trauma, she became able to express some of her feelings. She was enraged at her parents for not being able to accept her pregnancy. They just wanted to get rid of the problem. She also felt angry at Joe for not protecting her and the baby. Since it was her own parents who wanted the abortion, Joe put the blame back on Gina.

Gina had been in deep psychic pain and felt rejected. Caught between loyalties toward her parents, Joe, and her unborn child Gina was immobilized and unable to process her own feelings about the event. In a developmental sense she was stuck. She had not been given permission to grow up, have a baby, and become a mother. Her desire for independence and adulthood had been frustrated by her unsuccessful attempt to break the emotional reliance on her parents whom she loved and had always been so vital in her life. When she terminated the pregnancy, it was not only her pregnancy that was aborted; her embryonic womanhood had been aborted too. The result of the abortion was that she had become emotionally immobilized and uncertain. The loss of her child was an unprecedented assault on her sense of identity. Because she could not carry out the role of a protective mother, she felt an extraordinary sense of failure, and a deep sense of being violated. In a state of severe depression, Gina was incapable of making decisions, powerless to assert herself, and unable to love.

Despite his abusive behavior, Gina clung to her boyfriend Joe. His mistreatment of her confirmed her low self-esteem and sense of powerlessness. Moreover, she knew her parents hated him. By forcing her parents to accept Joe, she was him and was unconsciously lashing back punishing them by forcing her parents to accept -- echoing they way they had forced her to accept an unwanted abortion. This dynamic gave her a sense of control, yet his being a part of her life. Gina was trapped in a vicious cycle by which she was punishing both herself and her father.

Perhaps most important of all, Joe signified her connection to their aborted baby. Gina feared that giving him up would destroy the only bond remaining to the child she still needed to grieve. If she gave up Joe she would have to give up the hope of recreating the baby for whom she still needed to grieve.

Gina was trapped in a vicious cycle by which she was punishing both herself and her father.

Once Gina was in treatment for post-abortion trauma, she was able to express these feelings. It was important for both her sake and her family, however, that her parents should also enter into the therapy process with her. She needed them to validate her loss and accept their responsibility for contributing to her emotional devastation. Without this recognition deterioration otherwise their relationship could never be fully healed.

In entering into this family counseling situation, I knew each parent would attempt to justify and defend their actions as they struggled with their daughter's experience. This resistance or inability to confront and admit emotional or spiritual pain is called denial. In this phase of treatment, denial is a powerful temptation.

Gina's mom came first. She listened to her daughter and expressed sorrow. I watched a pained expression on the woman's face that persisted along with the inevitable but...

I know you are hurting BUT we thought we were doing the best thing. I realize this is hard BUT you must get on with your life. You wanted the baby BUT how would you ever pay for it? BUT how would you finish school. BUT, BUT, BUT...

The list goes on and on like dirty laundry, never ending, never finished. Each exception robbed Gina of the gift of fully acknowledging her loss. Her parents could not accept the pregnancy; now they couldn't accept her grief. She felt utterly rejected.

Father Knows Best?

Gina's father had no idea what she had sacrificed in order to please him. It was important for her to tell him, so Mr. Davis was invited for a session. The night before our meeting, he called me.

"My stomach has been upset all week since I heard about this meeting," he said. "I want to do what is best for Gina." Then his tone became more formal and forceful: "I just want you to know that this is NOT a moral issue to me. Gina had to have that abortion! I still think we made the right decision. If I had it to do again, I would choose the same thing. I know this is not what she wants to hear. Should I lie about it to make her feel better? Is that what I should do? Tell her I made a mistake? I cannot do that!"

With renewed determination, I explained, "Mr. Davis, I know you love your daughter very much. I know that she loves you or she never would have consented to have an abortion. The fact remains that your daughter lost something. What she lost was a child. Her baby; your grandchild. Gina thinks about it every day. She cries about it every night. The event is far from over for her. You need to hear how the abortion has affected her."

Mr. Davis did not respond. With conviction, I continued, "When someone dies, the worst thing another can say is "it was for the best, it's better this way." This does nothing to comfort and console; it only makes the person angry because you are not appreciating their loss or grief. Worse for Gina is that you do not recognize the life that she is missing. Gina misses her baby, a child you have not been able to acknowledge."

Eventually, Mr. Davis agreed that he would try to listen and that maybe he had something to learn. I really couldn't hope for more than that.

"Men are not prone to emotional mushiness," he reminded me. He honestly wished he could feel sorrow and compassion over the baby, but he could not. Nevertheless, he would listen if it would help his daughter.

Listening and Taking Responsibility

When Mr. Davis came in the next morning, he opened with a surprising statement. "I had no right to make that choice," he said. After wrestling with various points in our conversation all night, he admitted that for the first time he realized that abortion was not Gina's choice.

The session began and it was very intense. Gina expressed her anger, hurt and feelings of rejection. She also shared her grief about the aborted baby.

Mr. Davis began to face some things for the first time. He was finally able to consider the baby and to separate Joe from the pregnancy. Abortion was a way to scrape out any symptom of his daughter's sexual activity and heroically free her from the consequences of her own actions. He began to realize that his daughter was a woman now, one he should not have tried to control. He needed to trust Gina to be capable of making her own decisions without the threat of abandonment.

As these interpretations became clear to Mr. Davis, denial could no longer sustain its powerful grip. Suddenly grief came upon Mr. Davis. He stared in disbelief, as if a light had abruptly cast shocking rays into a blackened room.

His voice broke with anguish. "Oh my baby, my sweet baby, my Gina," he cried. "I am so sorry. I was so wrong." He pressed his face against her cheek and the tears finally came. His tears mingled with Gina's as they both wept. Gina put her arms around him. They embraced tightly as her father gently stroked her long hair. All the anger, the bitterness, the pent-up emotions, the grief, gave way. They sobbed in each other's arms. He begged for her forgiveness. Between tears and tissues, he told Gina she would have been an incredible mother. In one beautiful moment, her motherhood had been validated and Gina wept with relief.

In a subsequent joint session with her parents, Gina expressed her anger, hurt and feelings of rejection and shared her grief about the aborted baby. Gina also took personal responsibility for having allowed the abortion to occur and wanted her parents to do the same. This time, her parents listened without defending or rationalizing what had happened.

Therapy helped Gina's parents to understand the grave mistake that they had made in forcing Gina to choose between them and her baby. I encouraged them not to make her choose again between them and Joe. In bitterness and grief, Gina might permit another type of abortion: a termination of her role as their daughter.

By acknowledging Gina's grief, and sharing it with her, Mr. and Mrs. Davis restored their relationship with their daughter. Gina's loving and happy personality was eventually able to bloom once more. She could continue forward, was once again able to renew in her journey toward becoming a confident and capable adult. With the support of therapeutic intervention she found that she was able to identify her own needs -- like the desire to break up with Joe, and to attain her own goals.

Letters from Fathers To Their Children

Dear Angelina,

I am writing this letter to let you know that I have not forgotten you. You would be five years old today. I see you with long dark hair and a brilliant smile with a pink bow in your hair.

Your mother and I are so sorry we made the decision to abort you. I know that you forgive us, but that does not take away the feelings of regret. At first, I did not want to remember you. I had no regard for your memory and just blanked out the whole event. Over the last year, barely a day goes by without a thought of what could be. Every time I see a couple with a small child I think of you. When I see a new childrens movie, I think of how great it would have been to take you. When I see a commercial for Disney World, I think of how I will never see your face light up at the view of Cinderella's castle. When I see a pregnant mother, I think of you. I think of all the things and places I will never get to show you.... your first sunrise, your first flower, your first steps, your first words, your first hug from me and the sound of your voice shouting..."Daddy is home" when I get home from a long day. And most of all the ability to give you unconditional love as a parent should, unlike the love I received.

Through this weekend retreat I know you are o.k. and that you are with Jesus and all the other children waiting for Mommy and me, so you can one day give me that hug and say "Daddy is home".

Love Always,
Your Dad

Dear Danny,

I have blocked you out of my life for so many years. It's hard to believe that you would of been in your late 30's, the oldest of my children, the big brother to your three sisters. They have missed out and indeed have I. I never played ball with you or threw a football around like my dad & I had. I missed all those joys and I am sorry you have too. The next time I hear from your Mom, I'll tell her about this maybe she'll even want to come to a retreat like this one. I want to tell you why I picked this name of Daniel for you. When I was born my parents, my birth parents gave me away. I was Blessed Danny because I got great parents who took great care of me. I found out I was adopted just about the time I found out about you. Many yrs later your grandmother told me a story but let me tell you another story first. I have a puppy named Danny, actually Danny is getting quite old for a dog. There was a time in my life a time when I thought I had forgotten you, when I had a series of dreams. In these dreams I was in some type of group therapy about the death I caused to my dog Danny. I woke up confused and grief stricken... Well my son, a few years after that your grandma told me that my birth name, my baptized name was Daniel. I haven't been able to give you anything in this life my son, but at last, I have given you my name. I know you're in the hands of Jesus Daniel and I look for the day when I can hold you!

All my Love,
Your Daddy
Rachael's Vineyard Retreat
Sunday March 2007

Forbidden Grief
The Unspoken Pain of Abortion
By Theresa Karminski Burke with David Reardon (Acorn Books).

Recognizing abortion as a trauma in a person's life, this compelling work uniquely examines the psychological impact of induced abortion. It reflects in-depth insight and clinical examples of how an abortion may affect one's self-concept. It includes dozens of vignettes with psychological interpretation, excerpts from women's diaries and letters. It will validate the feelings of loss and shame experienced by many - presenting a name for their pain and helping them make sense of the 'self-destructive behaviors which often follow abortion.

For the clinician, *Forbidden Grief* provides a detailed explanation of how feelings, emotions and even psycho-physiological symptoms are related to abortion trauma through eating disorders, anxiety and panic responses, depression, and conflicts with maternal identity. Further, abortion itself may re-enact the trauma of former sexual abuse. These are important concepts to be aware of when dealing with post-aborted women and men. It can help them to understand self-destructive tendencies that often unconsciously follow trauma. This book will give you a detailed understanding of post-abortion symptoms and the many levels of traumatic impact.

Rachel's Vineyard
A Ministry of Priests For Life
www.RachelsVineyard.org
1-877-HOPE-4-ME
<u>**Weekend Retreats and Support Groups**</u>
<u>**for Healing After Abortion**</u>

National Office: 808 N. Henderson Rd.
                          King of Prussia, PA 19406
                          (ph) 610-354-0555 (fax) 610-354-0311

An Invitation for Healing…
   Rachel's Vineyard is a safe place to heal hearts broken by abortion. Weekend retreats offer you a supportive, confidential, and non-judgmental environment where women and men can reconcile painful post-abortive emotions and begin the process of healing.
   Rachel's Vineyard creates a place where men and women can share, often for the first time, their deepest feelings about abortion. You are allowed to dismantle troubling secrets in an environment of emotional and spiritual safety.
   Rachel's Vineyard is therapy for the soul. Participants, who have been trapped in anger towards themselves or others, experience forgiveness. Peace is found. Lives are restored. A sense of hope and meaning for the future is finally re-discovered.
   If you or someone you know is in need of post-abortion healing, we invite you to look at our website, ***www.RachelsVineyard.org****, to find a retreat site near you and continue your healing journey. You are also welcome to call our hotline,* ***1-877-HOPE-4-ME*** *to get in touch with your local Rachel's Vineyard site leader.*

About Rachel's Vineyard
   Rachel's Vineyard offers weekend retreats and support groups for spiritual and emotional healing after abortion held in over 200 sites worldwide. The program continues to expand internationally, with retreats in Africa, Australia, New Zealand, Canada, Portugal, Ireland, England, Spain, Italy, Korea, Poland, Taiwan, and South America.

The curriculum has been translated into French, Spanish, Portuguese, and Russian, with Flemish, Korean, Japanese, Italian and Chinese translations forthcoming.

Rachel's Vineyard offers clinical training and seminars to educate mental health professionals, clergy, and lay people about the effects of abortion. Continuing Education Credits are available. If you are interested in bringing a clinical training to your area, please contact Rachel's Vineyard Ministries at 610-354-0555.

Post Abortion Healing Resources

Rachel's Vineyard Ministries
Weekend Retreats for healing after Abortion
www.rachelsvineyard.org
1 877 HOPE 4 ME

Fatherhood Forever Foundation
Jason Baier Founder. Fatherhood Forever Foundation is dedicated to helping men find healing and hope after abortion by creating awareness that abortion does have an impact on men and providing encouragement and resources to those seeking help.

Web: www.fatherhoodforever.org
Email: fffinfo@fatherhoodforever.org
602 334 7651

Project Rachel
Project Rachel is the name of the Catholic Church's healing ministry to those who have been involved in abortion.
Web: www.hopeafterabortion.com
Email: noparh@juno.com

Healing A Father's Heart: A Post Abortion Bible Study for Men
By Linda Cochrane and Kathy Jones
Practical information to help hurting men work through the stages of post-abortion syndrome and find comfort in the reassurance of God's love and acceptance.

Men and Abortion-A Path to Healing
By Catherine Coyle, Ph.D.
This new study is the only pro-life book ever written specifically for men who have been hurt by a personal involvement with abortion. It focuses on the specific problems experienced by post-abortion men, including anger, helplessness, guilt, relationship problems and grief.

Printed in the United States
78563LV00005B/208-348